THE CALL,
THE ELECTION,
YOUR PURPOSE

THE CALL, THE ELECTION, YOUR PURPOSE

by DR. JOHN TETSOLA

END TIME WAVE
PUBLICATIONS

Bogota, New Jersey

The Call, The Election, Your Purpose

ISBN 0-889389-13-7

Unless otherwise indicated, all Scripture quotations are from the King James Version of the Bible. Scripture quotations marked (NIV) are taken from the HOLY Bible, NEW INTERNATIONAL VERSION ®, Copyright © 1973, 1978, 1984 by International Bible Society. Used by permission of Zondervan Publishing House. All rights reserved.

The "NIV" and "New International Version" trademarks are registered in the United States Patent and Trademark Office by International Bible Society. Use of either trademark requires the permission of International Bible Society. Scripture quotations marked (AMP) are taken from The Amplified Bible, Old Testament, Copyright © 1965, 1987 by the Zondervan Publishing House. The Amplified New Testament, Copyright © 1954, 1958, 1987 by The Lockman Foundation. Used by permission.

Those marked (NASB) are from the New American Standard Bible, Copyright© 1960, 1962, 1963, 1968, 1971, 1972, 1973, 1975, 1977 by The Lockman Foundation, La Habra, California. Used by permission.

Verses marked (TLB) are taken from The Living Bible, Copyright © 1971. Used by permission of Tyndale House Publishers, Inc., Wheaton, Ill. 60189.

Note:In some Scripture quotations, italics have been added by the author for emphasis only.

CONTENTS

DEDICATION

This book is dedicated to my beautiful wife, Vickie Tetsola, who co-pastors Ecclesia Church International with me. Vickie, I am very greatful for your tremendous help, your love, your strength and your never-ending depth of dedication to me personally and the ministry God entrusted me with. You have made it easy for me to accept the call, the election and my purpose for life. I love you dearly.

INTRODUCTION

Did you know that before you were born into this world, God had you on His mind? (Jer. 1:4-5). In fact, the most thought-out detail of creation was your life. God created you perfectly suited to fulfill a unique purpose.

As Christians, we know we are not here by accident. God has a specific mandate and assignment upon each of our lives. And in our journey to that end, He has given us specific callings at different times and places. These words-- calling, purpose and election--have long been overused and misunderstood by the Church. Used in a broad, sweeping context, they often seem too lofty and vague to hold real meaning in our everyday lives.

In the following pages, these powerful terms will be illuminated in a life-changing way. You will learn how they apply specifically to your life both personally and corporately in the Body of Christ. We are here to fulfill the mandate of God, and when we fully understand what this means, we will live happy and fulfilled lives. It will motivate and encourage you in every season of experience.

Like the Apostle Paul in II Tim. 4:7, we must fight for the destiny God has placed upon our lives. We must fight the temptation to be discouraged or weary rather than pressing diligently toward the finish. You may need to rid your land of some giants before receiving the promise of

God. You will need to pursue the anointing that is necessary to fulfill your mandate.

Your divine revelation of God's mandate can be used as a potent weapon that will thwart any evil the enemy has planned. Knowledge of what you are supposed to do will protect you from a seducing spirit and from doing something you are not supposed to--even when it looks good.

In II Peter 1:10, Peter says "know your election." Your election is what you are predesigned to become--but are not there yet. You can be elected as a prophet, a pastor or evangelist. But what kind of prophet, pastor or evangelist you are is determined by your calling. That is always where the specific is given. If you stay within your call and your election, and serve them faithfully, God promises an opened door to abundance in His Kingdom.

In this book, you will learn how to stay focused on your mandate and sidestep the strategies of the enemy. You will also discover that there are some things you are not to be involved in: the forbidden fruit of your call. They may be good things, but if they are not part of your calling, they are not God things, and will be detrimental to you.

You are only effective when your eyes are trained on your goal and when you stay within the boundaries of your call. Just as He gave Joshua distinct boundaries in the Promised Land, God always gives us a limiting line of function.

Within these pages, you will find many golden nuggets of truth that will dramatically impact your life.

You'll learn the secret of a successful ministry, hidden in the life of King Uzziah and his mandate from God. You'll be challenged by Elisha's willingness to serve, Joseph's journey to the palace and David's ability to sing praises to God in the midst of his enemy.

Most importantly, in the discovery of your own purpose and election, you will become increasingly formed and molded to the image of Christ. Yes, there may be pain and discomfort along the way, but God's voice will come to you in every season of life.

Don't settle for any less than God's best. Determine to stay the course and receive all that He has planned for you!

Dr. John Tetsola
July 1997

Chapter One

WHAT IS YOUR MANDATE?

In the mean while his disciples prayed him, saying, Master, eat.

But he said unto them, I have meat to eat that ye know not of.

Therefore said the disciples one to another, Hath any man brought him ought to eat?

Jesus saith unto them, My meat is to do the will of him that sent me, and to finish his work.

Say not ye, There are yet four months, and then cometh harvest? behold, I say unto you, Lift up your eyes, and look on the fields; for they are white already to harvest.

And he that reapeth receiveth wages, and gathereth fruit unto life eternal: that both he that soweth and he that reapeth may rejoice together.

                    John 4: 31-36

1

**And say to Archippus, Take heed to the ministry which
thou hast received in the Lord, that thou fulfil it.**
Colossians 4:17

Many people never discover the purpose God has for
their lives. They live all their lives unfulfilled. Not
untalented. Not ungifted. But unfulfilled because they do
not discover their personal destiny.

Some may find their destiny, but are unwilling to fulfill
or serve it with strength.

Three words have been highly misunderstood in the
Church. These words are *callings, elections* and *purposes.*
In the plan of God, these words are quite different. It is
absolutely important that we understand what they mean
and the roles they play in the fulfillment of the mandate of
God upon our lives.

Your callings plus your elections and your purpose
equals the *mandate.* So when we talk about the mandate of
God upon our life, we are referring to the calling, the
election and the purpose. It encompasses all of what God
intends for us to do.

The word *mandate* means an order, a command or an
assignment. Each of us is allocated an assignment that must
be fulfilled. We must find this assignment, follow it and
complete it. We have an assignment and our assignment is
hidden in our call, our election, and in our purpose.

2

But not only does this word refer to an assignment, it carries with it the connotation of a time frame. It is defined by time. In short, you don't have any time to waste in fulfilling the order or the assignment given to you by God. You cannot afford to postpone or delay the assignment of God upon your life and your ministry. You don't have time. When you find it, you must serve it or follow it with all of your energy.

Jesus said in verse 35 of John, chapter 4, "it is still four months until harvest time comes." There are time periods that are allocated to our mandate. We are not meant to be on this earth forever. We must walk circumspectly, redeeming the time.

THREE TYPES OF MANDATE

There are three types of mandate. There is the *personal* mandate, the *corporate* mandate and the *regional* or *territorial* mandate.

The *personal* mandate is the very assignment— the calling, the election and the purpose God has given to you as an individual person. This is exactly what God has purposed for our lives to embark on. One person's assignment is quite different from another. You can never compare your assignment with mine or mine with yours. The *corporate* mandate is the mandate that God has ordained for you in conjunction with others. It may be with a ministry, a group or a church. In this mandate, God expects you to plug your assignment into the main socket

3

of either the group, church or ministry that you are a part of. But when you plug your personal assignment into the corporate assignment of the church or ministry, you see your personal assignment fulfilled and also you see the corporate assignment fulfilled. The *regional* or territorial mandate is the mandate that God gives to you concerning a specific region or territory. God wants you to find this mandate, whether personally, corporately or regionally. He wants you to begin it, to follow it with intensity and momentum, and He wants you to finish it well.

For we are his workmanship, created in Christ Jesus unto good works, which God hath before ordained that we should walk in them.
Ephesians 2:10

Before He made heaven and earth, God ordained our destiny. He has specific assignments upon our lives. We are not here holding on. We are not here trying to get by. We are not just trying to make a living. We are here to fulfill the mandate of God. We are here to fulfill destiny with strength. We are here to fulfill purpose. And we are living in the right place, at the right age and at the right time.

FOCUS ON FINISHING

But watch thou in all things, endure afflictions, do the work of an evangelist, make full proof of thy ministry.

For I am now ready to be offered, and the time of my departure is at hand.

4

I have fought a good fight, I have finished my course, I have kept the faith:

Henceforth there is laid up for me a crown of righteousness, which the Lord, the righteous judge, shall give me at that day: and not to me only, but unto all them also that love his appearing.
II Timothy 4:5-8

When you catch the vision of the purpose that God saved you and placed you here on earth, you are automatically in sync with life and you become a fulfilled person at that moment. And when you catch the vision, God expects you to start with strength.

Many Christians are great starters, but they are not great finishers. God wants us to become finishers of what we have started. We must train ourselves and train our children concerning finishing whatever we put our hands to do.

Paul made a strong declaration here. Not only did he serve the mandate of God upon his life, he declared in verse 7, "I have fought the good— the worthy, the honorable and the noble— fight. I have finished the race and I have kept— firmly held— the faith." He saw the mandate as a worthy, honorable and noble assignment.

How do we look at what God has called us to do? Is it honorable and noble to us? You can only fight tenaciously for a thing that you believe is worthy and

5

honorable. We must learn to see God's assignment upon our lives as noble and honorable, and then fight to keep it.

When you find out the assignment of God upon your life, you must be determined to finish it. Some people find out the mandate upon their life but refuse to follow it. They want to do something other than what God called them to do. Others don't finish because they lack faith or knowledge, because of sin, because they neglect their body, or because they die early.

You may have to fight the good fight of faith to realize your destiny. When God gave the children of Israel the land, it was their inheritance— but the land had giants in it and they had to fight to get rid of the giants. You, also, will have giants residing in your destiny and you will have to fight to drive them out.

DESTINY IS A FIGHT

Jesus saith unto them, My meat is to do the will of him that sent me, and to finish his work.
John 4:34

I have fought a good fight, I have finished my course, I have kept the faith:
II Timothy 4:7

Anything that you are believing God for, that He said He would do, will result in a fight. You cannot be a Christian and be a passivist. You will get your brains beaten out.

In John 4:34, Jesus says, "My meat [my soul satisfaction] is to do the will of him that sent me and to finish his work." Notice, He did not say "my meat is to be famous." Nor did He say "my meat is to build a five-thousand church membership" or to "travel all over the world." But He says "my meat is to do the will of the Father and to finish the work."

We often pursue the by-products of the anointing or of the will of God, rather than pursuing the will of God. The fame, the travel and the five-thousand church membership are simply the by-products of those who are serving the will of God for their lives. Any man who truly serves the will of God for his life truly receives the benefit of the will of God.

The American church is very competitive. It is not about color. It's simply about competition. We see cross-overs in callings and in mandates because everyone wants quick and overnight successes. If the will of God is for you to build a small church in a small neighborhood, then be content with it. Serve it with all faithfulness.

Don't move from where God calls you because of pressure from church folks or because of the spirit of shame. Jesus was content with just serving the will of God for His life and He did it well.

The mega-church mentality has caused Christians and leaders to utilize every gimmick in the book to increase their church membership. Leaders sit around asking one another, "Doc, how many people did you pull in last Sunday?" Numbers to them are measured in how much money they can raise from the people. We even have ministers who will not come to certain churches, conferences or conventions if there is the absence of the large crowds. They want to know how many people will be present, all for the purpose of personal exposure and for finances.

I have found out, as a traveling minister, that the churches and ministers that bless me are not necessarily the large churches. In fact, the smaller churches and ministries tend to appreciate your anointing more, to hold your anointing in high esteem, and bless you financially than the large churches. I have heard other traveling ministers say the same thing.

Large does not mean strong. You can have a large ministry and yet have sitting on the pews weaklings who cannot drive out even one demon. On the other hand, you can have a membership of twenty, and demons are afraid to come anywhere near that service or building.

Now understand, there is nothing wrong with large churches. Churches are suppose to grow. If you are walking in the will of God, and you are a pastor, your church ought to grow. But don't be pressured to increase your church through gimmicks. Let the Spirit of God do it. Don't be pressured to act like the "big boys" if God has not given you the grace. As for traveling ministers, let God lead you to where you minister. Don't let your choice be influenced by the crowd or the finances.

Our food, our meat, our life source, the thing we live and breathe for should be to *do the will of God and to finish it*. Don't be concerned about the number of laps you make. More important is *whether you finish.* The New York Knicks basketball team often leads in the first three quarters, then fades off in the fourth quarter. Nobody cares how many laps you lead. It is how you finish that counts.

IGNORANT OF YOUR MANDATE

If you have problems understanding and embracing the mandate of God for your life, it is probably because of one or more of these three reasons:

1) You are confusing yourself with doubt and fear.

2) You are avoiding or rebelling against what you already know.

3) You are trying to do something you have not been called to do.

God is not hiding anything from us. He wants us to find the mandate for our lives. He wants us to follow it and He wants us to fulfill it.

SERVING YOUR ASSIGNMENT WITH STRENGTH

Then all the people of Judah took Uzziah, who was sixteen years old, and made him king in the room of his father Amaziah.

He built Eloth, and restored it to Judah, after that the king slept with his fathers.

Sixteen years old was Uzziah when he began to reign, and he reigned fifty and two years in Jerusalem. His mother's name also was Jecoliah of Jerusalem.

And he did that which was right in the sight of the LORD, according to all that his father Amaziah did.

And he sought God in the days of Zechariah, who had understanding in the visions of God: and as long as he sought the LORD, God made him to prosper.

And he went forth and warred against the Philistines, and brake down the wall of Gath, and the wall of Jabneh, and the wall of Ashdod, and built cities about Ashdod, and among the Philistines. And God helped him against the Philistines, and against the Arabians that dwelt in Gurbaal, and the Mehunims.

And the Ammonites gave gifts to Uzziah: and his name spread abroad even to the entering in of Egypt; for he strengthened himself exceedingly.

Moreover Uzziah built towers in Jerusalem at the corner gate, and at the valley gate, and at the turning of the wall, and fortified them.

Also he built towers in the desert, and digged many wells: for he had much cattle, both in the low country, and in the plains: husbandmen also, and vine dressers in the mountains, and in Carmel: for he loved husbandry.

Moreover Uzziah had an host of fighting men, that went out to war by bands, according to the number of their account by the hand of Jeiel the scribe and Maaseiah the ruler, under the hand of Hananiah, one of the king's captains.

The whole number of the chief of the fathers of the mighty men of valour were two thousand and six hundred.

And under their hand was an army, three hundred thousand and seven thousand and five hundred, that made war with mighty power, to help the king against the enemy.

And Uzziah prepared for them throughout all the host shields, and spears, and helmets, and habergeons, and bows, and slings to cast stones.

And he made in Jerusalem engines, invented by cunning men, to be on the towers and upon the bulwarks, to shoot arrows and great stones withal. And his name spread far abroad; for he was marvellously helped, till he was strong.

But when he was strong, his heart was lifted up to his destruction: for he transgressed against the LORD his God, and went into the temple of the LORD to burn incense upon the altar of incense.

And Azariah the priest went in after him, and with him fourscore priests of the LORD, that were valiant men:

And they withstood Uzziah the king, and said unto him, It appertaineth not unto thee, Uzziah, to burn incense unto the LORD, but to the priests the sons of Aaron, that are consecrated to burn incense: go out of the sanctuary; for thou hast trespassed; neither shall it be for thine honour from the LORD God.

Then Uzziah was wroth, and had a censer in his hand to burn incense: and while he was wroth with the priests, the leprosy even rose up in his forehead before the priests in the house of the LORD, from beside the incense altar.

And Azariah the chief priest, and all the priests, looked upon him, and, behold, he was leprous in his forehead, and they thrust him out from thence; yea, himself hasted also to go out, because the LORD had smitten him.

And Uzziah the king was a leper unto the day of his death, and dwelt in a several house, being a leper; for he was cut off from the house of the LORD: and Jotham his son was over the king's house, judging the people of the land.
                                        II Chronicles 26:1-21

This is the story of an incredible young king who got hold of the mandate of God upon his life and started it with vigor and zeal, but did not complete it. I believe this is a strong warning for the Church in this hour.

King Uzziah was just sixteen years old when he began to serve the assignment of God upon his life. He started well by doing everything right in the sight of the Lord. The Bible says in verse 5 that "he sets himself to seek God." That is always the secret of strength in serving the mandate of God, and "as long as he sought the Lord, God

12

made him to prosper." The word "sought" here does not just mean to "inquire of a thing." This word goes further to mean "yearned for." So, as long as King Uzziah yearned for the Lord with passion, God prospered him.

Uzziah struck the main cord for a successful ministry. A ministry is successful when the appointed man of the ministry is able to inquire of the Lord with yearning on a consistent basis. Not just when the ministry began. Not just when all hell breaks loose, but even in the times when the storm is calm and everything seems to be looking great.

As long as Uzziah yearned after God, God continually prospered him. Verse 8 says that he was such a mighty man that his enemies sent him gifts. He was very famous; in fact, so famous that his name was known at the entrance of the gate of Egypt.

> **And the Ammonites gave gifts to Uzziah: and his name spread abroad even to the entering in of Egypt; for he strengthened himself exceedingly.**
> **II Chronicles 26:8**

The "entering in of Egypt" means the gate of Egypt, the authority of Egypt. The kings of Egypt knew Uzziah. The leadership of the nation knew him. Egypt then was like what America is to the world today. This was a very blessed young man. God helped him as long as he knew who he was and who God was. God helped this young king as long as he knew where he stood, as long as he was dependent on God, as long as he was weak in his own sight, as long as he knew the hand of God.

God will do the same today. As long as we are dependent on Him, He will prosper us. He will back us up in all our endeavors. He will make certain that the very mandate upon our lives is fulfilled.

And God helped him against the Philistines, and against the Arabians that dwelt in Gurbaal, and the Mehunims.

And the Ammonites gave gifts to Uzziah: and his name spread abroad even to the entering in of Egypt; for he strengthened himself exceedingly.

Moreover Uzziah built towers in Jerusalem at the corner gate, and at the valley gate, and at the turning of the wall, and fortified them.
Also he built towers in the desert, and digged many wells: for he had much cattle, both in the low country, and in the plains: husbandmen also, and vine dressers in the mountains, and in Carmel: for he loved husbandry.

Moreover Uzziah had an host of fighting men, that went out to war by bands, according to the number of their account by the hand of Jeiel the scribe and Maaseiah the ruler, under the hand of Hananiah, one of the king's captains.

The whole number of the chief of the fathers of the mighty men of valour were two thousand and six hundred.

And under their hand was an army, three hundred thousand and seven thousand and five hundred, that made war with mighty power, to help the king against the enemy.

14

And Uzziah prepared for them throughout all the host shields, and spears, and helmets, and habergeons, and bows, and slings to cast stones.

And he made in Jerusalem engines, invented by cunning men, to be on the towers and upon the bulwarks, to shoot arrows and great stones withal. And his name spread far abroad; for he was marvellously helped, till he was strong.
II Chronicles 26:7-15

Look at the secret of his prosperity. The Scriptures above show us the great feats that God helped Uzziah accomplish. This man was more rich and famous than words can describe. But remember the secret. It was contingent on the fact that he was dependent on the strength of God. As long as he sought God, He prospered him.

And he made in Jerusalem engines, invented by cunning men, to be on the towers and upon the bulwarks, to shoot arrows and great stones withal. And his name spread far abroad; for he was marvellously helped, till he was strong.

But when he was strong, his heart was lifted up to his destruction: for he transgressed against the LORD his God, and went into the temple of the LORD to burn incense upon the altar of incense.
II Chronicles 26:15-16

Note what the Scripture says in verse 15..."for he was marvellously helped, till he was strong." As long as Uzziah was not dependent on his strength, God helped him. But then he began to feel strong, no longer needing the assistance of God.

And that generally spells the beginning of failure in whatever God calls us to do. This is a strong warning to leaders. I believe there are many leaders who began well, sought after God at the beginning of their mandate, watched their companies and their attitude, determined in their hearts to walk in integrity and character. But after they accomplished some things, after their faces were plastered on television, after all the doors swung open, after the church swelled to five thousand, they became strong. For they forgot when God marvelously helped them.

This was the exact predicament of Uzziah. Verse 16 says, "But when he was strong, his heart was lifted up to his destruction." God is still warning the Church today. The moment you become strong, you lose your dependability on God. And when you lose your dependability on Him, you have completely lost everything.

THE DESIRE FOR ANOTHER MAN'S CALLING

And Azariah the priest went in after him, and with him fourscore priests of the LORD, that were valiant men:

And they withstood Uzziah the king, and said unto him, It appertaineth not unto thee, Uzziah, to burn incense unto the LORD, but to the priests the sons of Aaron, that are consecrated to burn incense: go out of the sanctuary; for thou hast trespassed; neither shall it be for thine honour from the LORD God.

II Chronicles 26:17-18

When Uzziah lost his dependence upon God, he no longer reverenced the things of God. The fear he once had was gone. Now he was trying to be a priest when God called him to be a king. He was stepping out of his calling, his election and his purpose.

That is what usually happens when you lose your dependence on the strength of God. You make your own decisions, you choose whatever office or calling that suits you. You end up eating the "portion" that belongs to God.

This still is happening in the Church today. We have men that God marvelously helped, men who once had the fear of God, men who once walked in integrity and character, but now, like King Uzziah, have stepped into arenas and boundaries that were never allocated to them by God. Because they lack proper submission to the right authority, they are like a time bomb waiting to explode. Sadly, innocent lives will reap the consequences.

LOCKED UP AND LOCKED OUT

And they withstood Uzziah the king, and said unto him, It appertaineth not unto thee, Uzziah, to burn incense unto the LORD, but to the priests the sons of Aaron, that are consecrated to burn incense: go out of the sanctuary; for thou hast trespassed; neither shall it be for thine honour from the LORD God.

Then Uzziah was wroth, and had a censer in his hand to burn incense: and while he was wroth with the priests, the

17

leprosy even rose up in his forehead before the priests in the house of the LORD, from beside the incense altar.

And Azariah the chief priest, and all the priests, looked upon him, and, behold, he was leprous in his forehead, and they thrust him out from thence; yea, himself hasted also to go out, because the LORD had smitten him.

II Chronicles 26:18-20

Uzziah was not willing to receive correction from the priests. In fact, the Bible says he "was wroth" and he took the censer in his hand to burn incense. The censer belonged to the priests, not to Uzziah. But because his dependence upon God was gone, he was not afraid of what he did. And he payed dearly for it. He ended up becoming a leper.

Lepers were locked up and kept separate from people. That is what happens when you lose the fear of the Lord and your dependence upon him. You end up not just being locked up in your own world, but being locked out of the things of God and of the favor of God.

Chapter Two

SEVEN PRINCIPLES TO RECEIVING THE ANOINTING

For many are called, but few are chosen.
Matthew 22:14

How do you become chosen for a mandate? The Bible says that many are called, but few are chosen. This doesn't mean that God will point His finger at you and order you to submit. God will not force something on you. Rather, you must choose to follow. You choose to serve. If you choose, you will be chosen. The mandate of God is not easy...that is why only few are willing to accept it or embrace it.

Now when you become chosen, God will anoint you. There are two kinds of anointing that we receive. The first anointing is for your personal walk with Christ, the anointing you receive when you are first born again. This anointing allows you to live out successfully the Christian walk.

19

But when you become chosen to a particular assignment, you receive another anointing for that specific assignment upon your life, enabling you to execute that assignment. This second anointing and grace can only work on the mandate allocated to it.

And Jehu the son of Nimshi shalt thou anoint to be king over Israel: and Elisha the son of Shaphat of Abelmeholah shalt thou anoint to be prophet in thy room.

And it shall come to pass, that him that escapeth the sword of Hazael shall Jehu slay: and him that escapeth from the sword of Jehu shall Elisha slay.
I Kings 19:16-17

Looking at the life of the prophet Elisha, we can draw upon some dynamic principles regarding God's mandate upon our lives. We will learn why God anointed Elisha for His mandate, and why He will anoint us, also, for His mandate.

There are seven reasons why God will anoint you to fulfill His mandate.

And Jehu the son of Nimshi shalt thou anoint to be king over Israel: and Elisha the son of Shaphat of Abelmeholah shalt thou anoint to be prophet in thy room.
I Kings 19:16

The first reason why God anointed Elisha to fulfill his mandate was because he was CALLED and then he was CHOSEN. God spoke to the prophet Elijah to go and anoint Elisha because he was chosen.

20

When you are called and then you become chosen, God will anoint you for that assignment. You cannot fulfill your ministry without the anointing. If you ever want to fulfill the mandate upon your life, make sure you are anointed for the task.

Listen, O isles, unto me; and hearken, ye people, from far; The LORD hath called me from the womb; from the bowels of my mother hath he made mention of my name.

And he hath made my mouth like a sharp sword; in the shadow of his hand hath he hid me, and made me a polished shaft; in his quiver hath he hid me;

And said unto me, Thou art my servant, O Israel, in whom I will be glorified.

Isaiah 49:1-3

God was the one who called Isaiah from his mother's womb with the assignment upon his life. And because God called him, He put the word of the mandate in Isaiah's mouth. The words then became like a sharp sword capable of dividing, cutting and penetrating any barrier against the mandate.

In ancient days, if they did not polish the arrows that flew out of the bows, they would not stick to their targets. So God polishes you. He prepares you and lubricates you so that you can stick when you are sent, and so you can hit the mark with strength.

21

BEING A WARRIOR

And it shall come to pass, that him that escapeth the sword of Hazael shall Jehu slay: and him that escapeth from the sword of Jehu shall Elisha slay.
I Kings 19:17

Second, God anointed Elisha for the assignment because he was a warrior. He was skilled in the use of the sword. He was already in a training position. Often, we wait to get anointed before we do something. God is saying, get your hands busy and working for Me. He anoints people who are busy, not people who are waiting to be anointed.

BEING A WORKER

So he departed thence, and found Elisha the son of Shaphat, who was plowing with twelve yoke of oxen before him, and he with the twelfth: and Elijah passed by him, and cast his mantle upon him.
I Kings 19:19

The third reason Elisha was anointed was because he was a worker. He was not lazy. He was willing to do anything. He was hard working. God will anoint us when we become workers and stop being lazy. Can you imagine plowing behind twelve yokes of oxen and all of them throwing dirt at you? Your clothes are filthy and your face is caked with mud.

The mantle came on Elisha while he was full of dirt. He had his heart in what he was doing. He was plowing with the yoke of oxen.

God does not choose men who are fit. He fits men who are chosen. You cannot make an able man faithful. But you can sure make a faithful man able.

BEING WILLING TO LET GO

And he left the oxen, and ran after Elijah, and said, Let me, I pray thee, kiss my father and my mother, and then I will follow thee. And he said unto him, Go back again: for what have I done to thee?

I Kings 19:20

The next reason Elisha was anointed was because he was willing to let go of what he had and where he was for something unknown but new. He was willing to forsake all. God will anoint us likewise if we are determined and willing to let go of what we have and where we have been for something fresh and new from Him.

Elisha came from a wealthy family that had twelve yoke of oxen. During his time, most farmers just had one or two yoke of oxen, but his father owned a large number of oxen.

And he returned back from him, and took a yoke of oxen, and slew them, and boiled their flesh with the instruments of the oxen, and gave unto the people, and they did eat.

I Kings 19:21a

The fifth reason God anointed him was that he was willing to renounce his former life and forget his past. Elisha was willing to burn up the farming instruments that he had been using. He was willing to forget the past and embrace what God had for him. Elisha was willing to forsake all, and willing to forget yesterday.

God will anoint us for that assignment upon our lives if we are willing to burn up those old farming instruments of our ideas, our strategies, our methods and then allow Him to arm us again with fresh instruments.

WILLING TO BE A SERVANT

Then he arose, and went after Elijah, and ministered unto him.

I Kings 19:21b

The next reason why God anointed Elisha to fulfill his mandate with strength was because Elisha was willing to become "ONE OF Elijah's servants." Not his first servant, but just one of the guys. He was not looking for notoriety or popularity. He did not care who saw him. All he was interested in was just being a part of this man and his ministry. He was willing to be "one of" and not "the."

In I Kings 18:43, we find that Elijah had more than one servant. He had another servant called Gehazi, who was with Elijah before Elisha's arrival. Elijah had a number of servants, and when Elisha showed up on the scene, he was willing to become just another servant. He did not have to be given a position. He was just satisfied being one of Elijah's servants.

This is a very important lesson we need to learn. God will anoint you only if you are willing to just be a part of what He is doing, not wanting to be the captain. If He promotes you to a captain's position, He will anoint you with the captain's anointing. But first of all, be willing to be "one of the servants" and not "the" servant.

Gehazi was not faithful and because of this, he was not a candidate for the double portion. Instead, Elisha received the double portion and Gehazi ended up serving Elisha.

Gehazi's true nature was revealed under the leadership of Elisha. He wanted fame. He wanted what he had not earned. He was deceptive and he paid dearly for it. Gehazi never got the anointing. He got the spirit of leprosy...while Elisha received the double portion.

BECOMING A FAUCET

But Jehoshaphat said, Is there not here a prophet of the LORD, that we may inquire of the LORD by him? And one of the king of Israel's servants answered and said, Here is Elisha the son of Shaphat, which poured water on the hands of Elijah.

II Kings 3:11

Finally, Elisha was anointed to fulfill the mandate upon his life because he was willing to become a FAUCET for the man of God. We must be willing to become faucets to others.

Elisha's job was to clean the man of God's hands. During ancient times, there were no faucets and because of the dust, when people returned home they washed their hands. Elisha's job was to go and get water from the well. When Elijah washed his hands, Elisha provided the "faucet." He was willing to be Elijah's faucet instead of being his daddy's rich little boy.

Chapter Three

THE DIFFERENCE BETWEEN
DESTINY AND PURPOSE

What is the difference between DESTINY and PURPOSE?

Destiny is the inevitable fate to which one is destined. You and I have been destined to some inevitable fate. It is not a bad fate. It is a good fate. It is your preordained portion. At the cross, there was a preordained portion for you as an individual, for you as a family, for you as a church, for you as a city. It was preordained that you will get a portion.

There is nothing worse than meeting a human being who does not know his destiny. That is why God is raising up prophets in this end time to reveal His destiny into the lives of God's people, so He can put in their hands a weapon to overcome the powers of darkness. Knowing your destiny is a powerful weapon.

Purpose, on the other hand, simply means "your role discovered." It is displayed in your role at an hour or at a season. Purpose is found in the reason for your circumstances... it's behind your objective in life.

Every purpose is established by counsel: and with good advice make war.

Proverbs 20:18

To every thing there is a season, and a time to every purpose under the heaven:

Ecclesiastes 3:1

Your purpose is discovered, not revealed. Destiny is revealed by God, but purpose is discovered by you. When God reveals your destiny to you, He never tells you the purpose of your destiny.

THE PIT, THE PRISON AND THE PALACE

Look at the example of Joseph. God revealed to Joseph in a dream his destiny of becoming a prime minister and people bowing before him. Excited by his dream, Joseph went around telling his brothers and friends about the revelation of his destiny.

Why didn't God tell Joseph about all that was to happen to him when he began to serve his destiny— the pit, wrong accusation and his impending prison experience? Because Joseph would have to discover it on his own, and this discovery would help make him become conformed to the image of God.

We are destined to be conformed to the image of Gc God wants us to resemble Him, and this resemblance comes as a result of being adjusted and molded. You can never receive the image of Christ without the adjustment of the Lord in your life. He has to adjust you to fit that portrait. If you understand this, you will begin to enjoy your Christianity. You will understand that whatever happens is not by chance, that God has His hand in it.

In your discovery of your purpose, you are being formed and adjusted on an ongoing basis to the image of Christ. God wants to form inside of us the image of His Son Christ Jesus and, on most occasions, it takes war to get there. You must be willing to war and fight for the image of Christ. The image of Christ can only be formed in you as you go through your Potiphar's house experience, as you go through your pit experience, as you go through your prison experience. The image is not formed from beautiful ingredients. It is always formed from experiences and ingredients that taste bitter.

Now take note of this. In the process of going through all these experiences, you are discovering your purpose. Purpose is never discovered in the palace. Purpose is only discovered on your *way* to the palace. Never despise the hours or seasons of sufferings. I am not referring to stupid things that we incur on ourselves. I am talking about sufferings that come because of your stand for Christ.

Get excited about these kind of sufferings. If you truly understand the purpose of the suffering and allow the Lord to move on your behalf, you will discover that the Holy Spirit will use it to mold you, to adjust you and to properly fine-tune you to resemble the image of Christ. The Scripture even makes it more exciting by saying that every time you suffer, you qualify for a greater joy.

FROM THE CAVE TO KING OF ISRAEL

Look at the example of David. One day Samuel arrives and anoints him, declaring that David is going to be the king of Israel. God did not say to David, "you are going to encounter Goliath," or "you are going to fight the Philistines." Why didn't God tell David all that was going to happen to him? Because he would have to discover his purpose as he journeyed toward his destiny. Praise is much more sweet when you learn to praise God when everything is going wrong.

David knew that one day he was going to be the king of Israel. While he was in a cave hiding from a jealous madman by the name of Saul, he still remembered that God had called him and elected him to be the king of Israel. And while in the cave running for his life, he was able to declare that his heart was fixed and he would sing praises. What an incredible posture to be taken by a man who is being pursued by his enemy! David declared the posture of his heart. He said his heart was fixed. In those moments of time in David's life, he was discovering his purpose.

FOCUS ON YOUR TOMORROW

Whoso keepeth the commandment shall feel no evil thing: and a wise man's heart discerneth both time and judgment.
Ecclesiastes 8:5

For every matter, there is a time and judgment. When God shows you your election and you go through your season or time of purpose in your life, remember that another moment or season of times and of judgment is coming after. Your phases in life are only seasonal. You must learn and determine to take your eyes from your now and put your eyes on your tomorrow.

Whatever you are going through, whether sickness, poverty or financial problems, it is only seasonal. The question is, *will you be able to survive your season?* The Bible says that Jesus was able to endure the cross for the joy that was set before Him. He saw what was beyond the cross. That is why He was able to survive the cross. You have to learn to look beyond the cross, beyond your present circumstances, to the election that God has set before you... and you will survive your season.

Ecclesiastes 8:5 says there is a season or a moment of time and a moment of judgment in your life. The word "time" means "a season of activity" and the word "judgment" means the verdict for that activity. During your phase or your time of purpose, you may make some mistakes and because of this, there is going to be a verdict or a judgment.

31

[But] he who commits sin [who practices evildoing] is of the devil [takes his character from the evil one], for the devil has sinned (violated the divine law) from the beginning. The reason the Son of God was made manifest (visible) was to undo (destroy, loosen, and dissolve) the works the devil [has done].

I John 3:8 (AMP)

And Jesus answered them, saying, The hour is come, that the Son of man should be glorified.

John 12:23

Remember that the ultimate purpose of Jesus appearing on earth was to destroy the works of the enemy. Another translation says for this purpose was the Son of God manifested that He might destroy the devil's ability to work. The devil's ability to work in your life is over! He can suggest things and you can believe them. But his ability to work in your life is over.

But for this benefit to become our portion, Jesus went through seasons and hours of purpose. In verse 23 of the above Scripture in John, we see that Jesus knew exactly what was supposed to be happening at that hour in His life. The contradiction to this verse is that Jesus said that "the hour to be glorified has arrived." Now this is interesting because in a few verses after that, He says that His soul is troubled. How can He say His soul is troubled when He just told us that the purpose of this hour is for Him to be glorified?

He says further, what then shall I say about it? In other words, how do I respond? Then He answers it for Himself. He says, must I say Father save me from this hour? No. Instead He says, for this purpose I came to this hour.

Jesus was vexed. The word "vexed" means to perplex the mind by suggesting doubts about your destiny. This always is what the enemy does when you are just about to be glorified in the hour of your purpose.

Jesus was about to be glorified. Suddenly Satan came and vexed His soul and perplexed His mind by suggesting doubts about His ultimate eternal calling and destiny by saying He was not going to make it. I don't know what Satan said to Jesus. Perhaps he said, "you are not going to make it beyond the cross." And Jesus, like you and I, was vexed. He wondered what to do with the perplexing of the mind. Should He pray "Father save me from this hour"? No, He does not want to be saved from that hour because that is the hour of His glorification. Rather, Jesus said for this reason and for this purpose I have come for this hour.

In other words, the reason and the purpose of coming to the hour is not to say, God get me out of this hour, but instead, this hour is supposed to take me into the next dimension of my life which is to be glorified. Jesus knew this and we have to know this.

When you know you are on the verge of striking it rich, when you know you are about to be healed, and when you know God is about to raise you up and do what He says He would do, Satan will come and vex your soul. This is when we need to stand up and say, I don't want to be saved from this hour. I am going to go through it. I am going to fight. Do you know what will happen? God will communicate with you by His Spirit and when He does, He is going to glorify His Name.

During the hour when you are trying to discover your purpose, Satan will perplex your mind with doubt, just when you are about to arrive at your destination. As the enemy begins to vex your soul, you are going to be tempted to take your life, to abandon the assignment of God upon your life. *But you must determine to stay on your course with the Word of the Lord.* Don't ever wish to be saved from that hour. Because when you are saved from it, you are not going to get to your election.

The weapon to survive this hour is the weapon of *praise.* Begin to praise and thank Him for the hour. As you begin to truly praise Him, a voice of assurance will come to you to reassure you that He will glorify you again. God's voice will come to you in every season of your life. He will not change His mind. His voice will bring you out of one hour or season and take you into the next hour or season of your life. During your darkest moment, if you can lift up your hands to God and say "I glorify Your Name," the voice of the Father will come to you and deliver you from your season of battle and from the vexation of Satan's power.

Chapter Four

IDENTIFYING YOUR CALL AND ELECTION

There is a big difference between the call upon your life and the election of God on your life. Many have misunderstood the call for the election and the election for the call. It is very important that we understand this in the realm of the spirit and then to bring this understanding into our daily walk.

It is the Father's will that gives you access to the kingdom of God. If God says that you are to be an evangelist and you decide to go into the business world, it means that you are out of the will of God, doing good works but touching something forbidden. You must understand that *good* is not always *God*. A good work done under false pretense is not the Spirit of the Lord. Blind obedience is very dangerous.

There are forbidden trees that are planted in everyone's life. There also are forbidden regions in everyone's life. You need to find your forbidden tree and your forbidden region. What may create life to you may create death to me. You must always make certain that you are not eating the forbidden fruit in your life.

There are things at this point in your life that are forbidden to you. You may be forbidden to be a pastor, an evangelist or even a businessman. You must find out what you are forbidden from and be willing to stand against it. Make up your mind not to defile yourself.

YOUR SECRET WEAPON

At midday, O king, I saw in the way a light from heaven, above the brightness of the sun, shining round about me and them which journeyed with me.

And when we were all fallen to the earth, I heard a voice speaking unto me, and saying in the Hebrew tongue, Saul, Saul, why persecutest thou me? it is hard for thee to kick against the pricks.

And I said, Who art thou, Lord? And he said, I am Jesus whom thou persecutest.

But rise, and stand upon thy feet: for I have appeared unto thee for this purpose, to make thee a minister and a witness both of these things which thou hast seen, and of those things in the which I will appear unto thee;
Acts 26:13-16

God has given to every one of us a secret weapon that will withstand any attack from the enemy. That weapon is *a divine revelation knowledge of God's mandate.* Knowledge of what you are supposed to do will protect you from a seducing spirit, from doing what you are not supposed to do, even if it looks good. In Acts 26, verse 16, the Lord said to Paul in his conversion that "I have appeared unto thee for this purpose." Paul was mandated to understand why he was called. This understanding then produced a corresponding energy that enabled him to execute what God had ordered for his life.

> And we know that all things work together for good to them that love God, to them who are the called according to his purpose.

> For whom he did foreknow, he also did predestinate to be conformed to the image of his Son, that he might be the firstborn among many brethren.

> Moreover whom he did predestinate, them he also called: and whom he called, them he also justified: and whom he justified, them he also glorified.
>
> **Romans 8:28-30**

God predestined everyone of us to become something at a certain time in our lives. You must understand this. If you catch hold of this, you will be relaxed with yourself and with God and be content in serving the mandate of God upon your life.

In Romans, we learn that God predestined us to be conformed to the image of His Son. The word "predestination" is not something where God chooses somebody to be saved and some not to be saved. Predestination simply means "God marking out, God specifying a boundary of operation, to ordain you for a

37

specific region." In other words, when you were born, you may have been born for China, you may have been born for Africa or for Australia, or for England. Predestination helps you to define your marked regions of operation, your boundary of operation that was given to you or that was ordained before you were born.

When you are sure of this and are satisfied with it, you will be equipped with a tenacity that nothing from hell will stop you from entering into your purpose. But it takes the voice of God to give you the power to do it.

Predestination is a boundary of operation of authority that God preordains for you. When you are born, it is then released on your behalf. God has a specific time for the authority to be released. Even though sometimes it may take a period of time, the authority will still be released.

You may ask, what if I never find it or walk in it? Be assured, there is a promise that is released to you that will always remain in your household, whether you receive it or not. Without a promise, you are not going to get to your purpose.

HEARING THE VOICE OF GOD

The voice of God is often a thrilling thing to hear. But it is also the last comfortable day in your life. When God spoke to Moses and gave him His voice and His Word, it was the last comfortable day in his life.

Once you know your calling and your election and you walk in them, it becomes much easier to regularly hear the voice of God for your own life. As you become used to hearing the voice of God, your obedience level to the things of the Spirit begins to develop. Then God can trust you with others' elections and calls.

> **For though we walk in the flesh, we do not war after the flesh:**
>
> **(For the weapons of our warfare are not carnal, but mighty through God to the pulling down of strong holds;)**
>
> **Casting down imaginations, and every high thing that exalteth itself against the knowledge of God, and bringing into captivity every thought to the obedience of Christ;**
>
> **And having in a readiness to revenge all disobedience, when your obedience is fulfilled.**
>
> **II Corinthians 10:3-6**

Look at verse 6 of the above Scripture. It says "having a readiness..." That is, having practiced, having prepared and having done it in your own life. What? Obedience. In other words, God is saying I will let you minister on demonic power or the kingdom of darkness in somebody else's life. I will let you help them if they are in the state of disobedience, but first you must fulfill obedience in your own life.

39

WHAT IS AN ELECTION?

Wherefore the rather, brethren, give diligence to make your calling and election sure: for if ye do these things, ye shall never fall:

For so an entrance shall be ministered unto you abundantly into the everlasting kingdom of our Lord and Saviour Jesus Christ.

II Peter 1:10-11

An election simply means a promise made by an utterance. It has to do with your relationship with the Lord. You are elected by God's promise which was given to you through utterance. God must utter His promise to you concerning that assignment that you intend to embark upon.

When the word of promise is uttered to you, it is always vague and general. You don't just open the Bible to the Book of Jeremiah and say God told Jeremiah to go to Judah, so I will go to Texas. You cannot do that.

Instead, after God has told you what you are called to do, you can identify with a character in the Bible that walks in the same calling. If you have been called to be a prophet, then let God show you what kind of prophet He called you to be. You can be called as a Jeremiah-type prophet or an Isaiah-type prophet. Study that person and identify with him, then when you have done that, find out who you are *not*, before you tell people who you *are*.

40

And he confessed, and denied not; but confessed, I am not the Christ.

And they asked him, What then? Art thou Elias? And he saith, I am not. Art thou that prophet? And he answered, No.

Then said they unto him, Who art thou? that we may give an answer to them that sent us. What sayest thou of thyself?

He said, I am the voice of one crying in the wilderness, Make straight the way of the Lord, as said the prophet Esaias.

And they which were sent were of the Pharisees.

And they asked him, and said unto him, Why baptizest thou then, if thou be not that Christ, nor Elias, neither that prophet?

John answered them, saying, I baptize with water: but there standeth one among you, whom ye know not;

He it is, who coming after me is preferred before me, whose shoe's latchet I am not worthy to unloose.
                          John 1:20-27

When John the Baptist was asked "who are you?" he told them who he was NOT before he told them who he WAS. When God elects you to be something, find scriptures that will help you identify with that thing. You'll find it will help you through your hard times.

41

My favorite scriptures are those that deal with David's experience. That is why I preach so passionately about David. I have had the javelin of Saul thrown at me. I know what it is like to be driven out of the place— out of the sanctuary. So whenever anger rises up in me and the desire to avenge the Saul that hurts me, God stops me and tells me to go and study the life of David. I found out that David never attempted to kill Saul.

David had the power to destroy Saul. But what David did was to give that power which was in his possession back to God. God says vengeance is mine. Whenever you refuse to retaliate or destroy someone, what you are doing is giving back the power of destruction to God. When you surrender that power back to God, that is when God takes you to a higher level.

WHAT IS A CALL?

The word "call" in the Greek is *"kalieo"* which means "to incite by word." In other words, God will provoke you and He will stir you up. He will stir you to action. He will inflame you. He will excite and motivate you. I hear many people in the body of Christ saying they have a call, but they are lazy and unmotivated. They look and act like dead wood with no life.

The call of God is always the *detail* of your election. He will tell you where you are supposed to be a prophet and how you are supposed to operate. You are never provoked to action by your election. You are only

42

provoked to action by your call. In the election, the promise is vague. It is not specific. But the call is very specific. It provokes us to action.

God motivates you by His Spirit by giving you the details in your call. In II Peter 1:10, Peter says know your election (having an idea or a vague knowledge) and your call—the details of where you are called to—the regions, to what boundaries of operation, to what country, to your sphere of faith and to what set measure of rule. You can, for example, be elected as a prophet or as a pastor. But what kind of prophet or what kind of pastor you are is determined in your calling. That is always where the specific is given.

> Because of this, brethren, be all the more solicitous and eager to make sure (to ratify, to strengthen, to make steadfast), your calling and election: for if you do this you will never stumble or fall.
>
> Thus there will be richly and abundantly provided for you entry into the eternal kingdom of our Lord and Saviour Jesus Christ.
>
> **II Peter 1:10-11 (AMP)**

The word "stumble" in this Scripture is also the word "fall." But this has nothing to do with falling into sin. In the Greek, it means "never stop progressing." It means advancing or going forward.

In other words, if you know your calling and you are walking in it and you know your election and you are walking in it, the Bible says you will never stop progressing. You may sin, but you will never stop progressing.

You are always advancing. You will always go forward. Why? Because you are in your election and in your call. Even when you make a mistake, you get up and still continue progressing, even in your state of weakness. If you are diligent to stay in your calling and election, you will never stay down. You will always progress, even if you fall down or get hurt. Stay within your election. Stay within your call and you will never fall.

For the gifts and calling of God are without repentance.
Romans 11:29

The gifts and calling of God are without repentance. He does not change His mind. When a man of God falls into sin and he or she is not repentant and continues sinning, the call does not stop. The gift does not stop. But what is behind it comes to an end. For instance, a healing ministry is invalid without the commodity called compassion. Jesus was always moved by compassion and then He healed the multitude. The man of God that falls and remains in sin may continue in his gifting, still within his calling, still preaching and still praying for the sick. But in time, compassion begins to disappear, and finally his prayers for people are no longer driven by the spirit of compassion.

44

This is a point worth repeating. When you stay within your call and your election and you diligently serve them, you will always progress, even if you fall down. You may make mistakes or sin, but that does not mean the call and the election will be taken from you. All you need to do is get up and repent and start moving with your election and call.

The election and the call of God upon your life is a progressive thing. You may go to Potiphar's house like the young Joseph and be accused of rape. But you will keep progressing, even though you may be unaware you are going forward.

You may be locked up in a prison for nearly a lifetime. But if you are diligent with that call and election, you will still go forward. You will never stop progressing because you are in your call, you are in your election and you are at the right place. And even though you think you are not making it, you are progressing. One day you wake up a prisoner and the next day you wake up a prime minister. That is what God does for you.

Make certain you understand your call. Know your election. Once you know it and once you understand it, you will never stop progressing. That is good news!

THE SUPPLY OF ENTRANCE

Wherefore the rather, brethren, give diligence to make your calling and election sure: for if ye do these things, ye shall never fall:

For so an entrance shall be ministered unto you abundantly into the everlasting kingdom of our Lord and Saviour Jesus Christ.

II Peter 1:10-11

This Scripture says if you stay in your election and your call, entrance will be supplied to you. An opening will be supplied to you. A door will be open to you.

Your calling changes. It does not remain stagnant. A call is not an election. An election is a definite set promise and a definite set anointing. God may call you as a prophet and then assign you to Texas. Then after two years, He may say to you, all right, you have completed your assignment in Texas and now I am calling you as a prophet to England. Your call progresses.

The danger arises when the call changes and you don't obey the progressive call of God which comes by present truth and present revelation. You can be in a call that is old and that has bypassed the boundaries of your life. And the result is that you are no longer operating under the Spirit. A call can change in locations and in regions, but your initial gifting would remain the same even though it may expand.

46

A DOOR INTO THE KINGDOM

For so an entrance shall be ministered unto you abundantly into the everlasting kingdom of our Lord and Saviour Jesus Christ.

II Peter 1:11

The kingdom here is not a place called heaven. People think that when they get saved and when they die one day, they will go into the kingdom. No. You are going to heaven when you die if you have accepted Christ as your Savior and Lord. The kingdom, on the other hand, is a place that is present. Right now and right here. At this very moment alive on this earth. It is simply God's way or God's method of doing things.

Paul says that an effective door is opened for us when we begin to walk diligently in our call and in our election. So when an abundant door is opened for you, it means you can enter the kingdom— God's way of doing things— and move in the dimensions of the kingdom. But often, in going into the kingdom and its dimensions, you will have to fight the adversary on the way.

These shall make war with the Lamb, and the Lamb shall overcome them: for he is Lord of lords, and King of kings: and they that are with him are called, and chosen, and faithful.

Revelation 17:14

There are three types of people in the kingdom. The called, the chosen and the faithful. Which one are you?

47

You cannot be faithful until you have been called. And when you have been called, you have to be chosen. How do you get chosen? When you accept the call. God does not immediately choose you. You choose to be chosen. When you are chosen and you stay within the boundaries of what you have been chosen to, faithfulness is produced in you.

There are degrees of God's anointing. There is the thirty fold, the sixty fold and the hundred fold. You attain all of these by access into the kingdom.

If you stay within your call and your election and serve them diligently, God promises a door will be opened abundantly for you in the everlasting kingdom. You have access to enter the kingdom and when you enter the kingdom, a higher degree of dominion and a higher degree of authority begins to operate in your life. If you are going to receive an authority in the heavenlies, there's a wickedness, a force, a rulership of evil that says you will not get what you desire. There is a force that will stand between you and what God promises you.

But when you resist the enemy and fight the enemy and overcome it, you attain a higher degree of kingdom authority. The problem that we are having today is from men and women who have compromised their calls and elections and refused to walk diligently according to God's divine blueprint for their lives. The consequence: all those who are under such a leader begin to operate in the same fashion. Multiplicity begins to happen. A genetic

48

duplication of the same spirit begins to operate among those who are under him. The only way the circle is broken or destroyed is when a "David" arrives on the scene.

These Davids may at this very important moment be enjoying intriguing fellowship with the Lord while disposing of a few lions and bears. These men don't care about their names being great. All they want to know is that one day God will take their experience with the bear and the lion and show a nation that a little stone can go a long, long way.

When you obey your call, you have only just begun a journey where you will be proven to be chosen for something great. God takes faithful people and puts kingly anointing upon their lives. God wants to be able to take us from the thirty fold, which is our calling, to sixty fold, which is when we are being chosen, and then to the hundred fold, where you become a faithful man.

Whenever God is about to do something big, He doesn't look only for those that are called or chosen, but for a faithful man on whose behalf He can make Himself strong and prove His might. A man who has proven himself to God when he was called, proven himself when he was chosen. Someone who stayed upright, stayed in prayer, stayed fasting.

God is raising up faithful people in this hour. But it all begins when you obey your call.

And we know that all things work together for good to them that love God, to them who are the called according to his purpose.

For whom he did foreknow, he also did predestinate to be conformed to the image of his Son, that he might be the firstborn among many brethren.

Moreover whom he did predestinate, them he also called: and whom he called, them he also justified: and whom he justified, them he also glorified.

Romans 8:28-30

When God speaks into you, there is a whole process of transfiguration that begins to take place. It is beautiful. When you have proven that you are operating and walking in your election and call, He chooses you out of your call into something higher.

In the kingdom of Israel there were very great men. But David was chosen out of his call. Your election may be a prophet to the nations. Your call may be to serve in areas of the ministry that you don't really love. Don't ever despise the operation and the limitation of your call. Keep your eye on your election and be diligent with your call. When you do this, a higher level of authority will begin to take place in your life.

As a pastor and a prophet of God, sometimes I go into a meeting, and after the teaching and preaching I start prophesying. At times I find myself calling out people that may not be faithful in the church, do not come to church regularly, and the Lord speaks to me to prophesy to them.

I may say, "God has called you to become a prophet or an evangelist." At that time, these individuals may not even be doing what they are supposed to do. Sometimes ministers who know them don't like hearing such a word, because they have already made a negative judgment of that individual.

But God sees things differently. What was spoken to the individual is their election. God ministered his election to this individual, and now He is going to call him, within the context of the election, to be faithful.

When God speaks, the first thing He speaks is to your election. After telling you your election, then he may give you the "bad" news .... and ask you to clean the bathroom of the church, to paint the walls of the church, to take the garbage out, to be an usher, to join the security ministry.

WALKING IN YOUR CALLING

And we know that all things work together for good to them that love God, to them who are the called according to his purpose.
Romans 8:28

We have often read this Scripture and misunderstood what the Spirit of the Lord is saying here. Just loving God does not qualify all things to work together for your good. Your love of God PLUS walking in the calling that is found in your purpose qualify all things to work together for your good.

No matter what goes wrong, it will work out for your good. The Bible says "and to those that are the called according to his purpose." Not according to our own purpose, but according to His purpose. In the Greek, it says "those who are walking according to the calling of His purpose."

What is purpose? Purpose comes with the call. Destiny comes with the election. Your election tells you your destiny, what you will ultimately become. Joseph was elected to be a prime minister. But he was called to the pit. He was called to Potiphar's house. He was called to the prison. Joseph could never have been the man he was, did what he did for his brothers and did what he did for Egypt and Israel, had he not gone through the pit, Potiphar's house, the accusations and the prison experience.

Purpose unfolds— destiny does not unfold. Destiny is revealed immediately. Purpose unfolds as you obey your call. Through whatever you are called to, you will find out the purpose for your election.

Have you ever gone through a crisis in your life and, at the time, you couldn't understand why? And then, two or three years later you find out why God allowed that experience. That is because purpose during that time was unfolded.

For whom he did foreknow, he also did predestinate to be conformed to the image of his Son, that he might be the firstborn among many brethren.
Romans 8:29

The Scripture says He predestined us to be conformed to the image of His Son. "Conformed" means to be jointly formed in the union of, companionship with, His Son. It simply means resemblance by shaping and adjusting.

God does not need to be adjusted. It is we who need to be adjusted and changed into His image. That is what conforming is. God wants us adjusted and shaped so that we can fit into His image and not our image. This happens after you have been predestined and your election comes. Then you begin to resemble Him by His shaping and His adjusting.

Moreover whom he did predestinate, them he also called: and whom he called, them he also justified: and whom he justified, them he also glorified.
Romans 8:30

You have been predestined. Your destination has been preset. It has been predesigned. God has said it. You are called. That is your destiny. It was destined long before you were born. Now what God does is get you there. He calls you to get to your destiny that He already preordained before you were born, before He began the earth. He preordained this, but He says to get there, you have to obey the call.

Look at verse 30b. It says who He called, He also justified. In the Greek, "justify" means to regard as innocent, just as if you have never sinned. If you obey the call, He will regard you as innocent when you make a mistake and He will use all things to work together for your good.

Does that mean I can do what I like? No. You will suffer if you do that. You will reap what you sow. But you will be regarded as innocent if you remain obedient to His call.

He also says that those He justified, He glorified. "Glorify" in this context means "to treat with dignity" or "to be treated as a dignitary full of honor." I don't know about you, but there is nothing more that I want from God than to be treated as a dignitary and with honor. Paul says that the suffering of this present time cannot be compared to the glory, that is, the dignitary status that will be revealed in us one day.

Chapter Five

ELECTION BY GRACE OR BY GOOD WORKS?

God speaks your election--that to which you are elected. He speaks it forth. The election always determines and reveals your destiny. But your call reveals your purpose.

Now there is a difference between your election and your call. The election is the big picture. Election is when God shows you the outcome of your life. You don't know the purpose for that outcome. You don't know why He called you to become a president of a nation or a prime minister.

When the prophet Samuel showed up on David's doorstep and said he was going to be the next king of Israel, David immediately knew his destiny. He knew his election, but he did not know his purpose. Purpose was discovered in the life of David during a process of time which, unfortunately, required a few javelins and a few battles. There is a war that takes place when a promise is given to you and when God communicates your election. Satan wants you to fail in your purpose.

God, by His Spirit, may speak to an individual and say "I have called you to be an apostle or an evangelist or even a prophet." God is giving that individual his election. The individual is elected to be an apostle or an evangelist. That is who he is predestined to become. But that individual may not have the character to handle the apostolic or the evangelistic call.

So God takes him through various calls in his life. He may call him to be a janitor, a deacon, a psalmist in the house. He will get the individual to serve first, and after he obeys these calls, the call becomes greater. We receive the thirty fold dimension before we receive the hundred fold dimension in our life.

> **Wherefore the rather, brethren, give diligence to make your calling and election sure: for if ye do these things, ye shall never fall:**
> **II Peter 1:10**

The Scripture says that we must make ourselves diligent to make our call and our election sure. The word "sure" means stable and strong. Peter says let your election and your call be stable, strong and solidified. Don't waver in what God calls you to do.

We must learn to stabilize our call and our election. Solidify it. Once we do that, we must keep our eyes on it.

Your election is the outcome of your life--what you are predesigned to become, but are not there yet. So why would God tell you what you are going to become in twenty-five years' time, or fifteen year's time? Why doesn't He rather take you through your call first?

He wants you to keep your eyes on what you are elected to do first, so that when you are in your call, you will not forget that it is only temporary. Your call is temporary. There are many calls in your life to produce many purposes, to produce and to build character in you so that when you get to your time of promotion, God will have formed enough character in you to handle the apostolic, to handle the evangelistic, to handle the teaching, to handle the church of three thousand members, to handle the business of a billion dollars. He has to tell you the outcome so He can drive you there, so that you can press towards some great mark of high calling.

GRACE VERSUS WORKS

When God elects you to a thing, understand that you did not get elected because of your good works. You did not get elected based on what you produced. Your works do not give you accepted favor in receiving your election. The truth is, before you were born, because of God's grace He elected you to become something at a certain time in your life. That election was made known in the heavens. Before you were born, Satan knew what you were elected to do.

That is the reason some of us were attacked even before we were saved. Satan knew there was an election that God had preordained long before you were born. He knew that if you could get to that place of divine election and that if you allow God to form enough character within you, you would kick his behind the moment you get to that high calling.

That is the joy of election. You did not deserve it. None of us deserved grace. It is not by works. Our election is as a result of grace.

Not as though the word of God hath taken none effect. For they are not all Israel, which are of Israel:
Romans 9:6

When you are elected for something, you must fulfill your purpose to get to your destiny. When you understand the difference between destiny and purpose, you will realize that your call is extremely important, whether it is sweeping floors for a season, whether it is being a salesman for a season or whether it is working in Wal-Mart. These assignments are not small--because they are leading you toward your great election.

YOUR PURPOSE ON EARTH

You are elected for something when you are born and then when you get saved, suddenly you hear the voice of God. However, God spoke long before you were born. He spoke into existence the very forces of life, light and love that are in the earth right now.

When you get saved, that is when you begin to *hear* Him. And when you hear the voice of God, suddenly you get a picture in your mind as to what you are elected to, what the destiny of your life is. Your purpose on earth is not just to go to heaven, but to press toward the mark of the high calling that is on this earth so that you will be able to accomplish something— change lives, release people from their bondage, touch the power of God and let other people feel the same power that you touch.

That is what we strive for and that is why our election was given to us. We know that when we get saved, we will go to heaven. We know that when we die we will meet Him in heaven, but God is calling us into destiny. People who know where they are going. God is looking for people who are willing to show forth His praise.

But ye are a chosen generation, a royal priesthood, an holy nation, a peculiar people; that ye should show forth the praises of him who hath called you out of darkness into his marvellous light:

Which in time past were not a people, but are now the people of God: which had not obtained mercy, but now have obtained mercy.

I Peter 2:9-10

The original meaning of this Scripture says that He, God, has called us out of darkness into His glorious light to show the world "what is praisable about God." In other words, God is looking for a people that will give the world a reason to praise Him.

59

Daniel was a typical example. When Daniel was thrown into the lions' den, the king had to look down and find that Daniel was not consumed--and *then* he declared the praises of God and proclaimed there is only one God. Sometimes, it takes a great supernatural intervention of God during your most difficult times for God to be praised. God called us out of darkness into His glorious light to show to the world what is praisable about God.

YOUR ELECTION IS ETERNAL

For so an entrance shall be ministered unto you abundantly into the everlasting kingdom of our Lord and Saviour Jesus Christ.
II Peter 1:11

God's purpose will be fulfilled in your life because of what He has elected you to do. His election stands. He will not change His mind. Then, the moment He speaks to you, you begin the journey of being called. You may have been elected as an apostle or a prophet to the nations. But initially, God will call you to a specific region, a specific country or specific neighborhood. And wherever it may be, you must be able to wake up with a smile on your face and walk with satisfaction, knowing that God did not make a mistake. You must be happy with where you are called. Get excited about it.

Understand that your calling is seasonal. Your election is eternal. So while you remain faithful to that region, that state or that specific nation, God has not forgotten your election, which is as a prophet to the nations. Your ultimate destination is the election, but before your election is achieved, God expects you to walk faithfully in your calling.

You may be called to minister in a specific area or be called to be a deacon or an usher until you arrive at the place where God elected you to be. God takes everything that you go through and uses it for your good.

Even so then at this present time also there is a remnant according to the election of grace.
Romans 11:5

As called and elected people, we must learn prophetic warfare. We must know how to war properly. That is, how to pray according to divine elections and callings. We must allow the Spirit of God to stir us to pray that we fulfill His purpose which is only for a season. It may be for just three months, six months, a year, or maybe seven years. However long it may be, we must learn to understand the purpose that is assigned to a season over our calls.

Child of God, hear me carefully. There is a purpose in an hour. There is a purpose in a day. There is also a purpose in a season. You must be able to understand the purpose of the hour or season to survive that hour or that season. If you do not understand what the purpose of your season is, you will not be able to survive the attack of that season.

ONLY BY GRACE

Even so then at this present time also there is a remnant according to the election of grace.

And if by grace, then is it no more of works: otherwise grace is no more grace. But if it be of works, then is it no more grace: otherwise work is no more work.

What then? Israel hath not obtained that which he seeketh for; but the election hath obtained it, and the rest were blinded

Romans 11:5-7

There is an election of grace. We are elected before we have any opportunity to do good works or to prove that we are good persons. God only works all things together for good at the counsel of His will. If you are doing His will and receiving His counsel, He works for you. When Christ died on the cross, He died so that you can fulfill a purpose in life. And God is always willing to reveal it to you.

Be not thou therefore ashamed of the testimony of our Lord, nor of me his prisoner: but be thou partaker of the afflictions of the gospel according to the power of God;

Who hath saved us, and called us with an holy calling, not according to our works, but according to his own purpose and grace, which was given us in Christ Jesus before the world began,

But is now made manifest by the appearing of our Saviour Jesus Christ, who hath abolished death, and hath brought life and immortality to light through the gospel:

Whereunto I am appointed a preacher, and an apostle, and a teacher of the Gentiles.
                                           II Timothy 1:8-11

In this Scripture, Paul tells us that he was appointed as a preacher, teacher and apostle to the Gentiles, not because he did something good or bad. But that before time began, Paul's name appeared in His heart and that when Jesus got on the cross, Paul's name was stored in His heart--and now that He is resurrected, He has given unto Him that Name that is exalted above any other name. That enables him to fulfill what God had originally ordained him to be.

Then the word of the LORD came unto me, saying,

Before I formed thee in the belly I knew thee; and before thou camest forth out of the womb I sanctified thee, [and] I ordained thee a prophet unto the nations.
                                           Jeremiah 1:4-5

Election of grace means you got elected without deserving it. Your work will never get you to your destiny. But it will get you to your purpose...through your time of calling. In the above Scripture, God says to Jeremiah, "... before I formed you in the womb, I knew thee and before thou cameth forth out of the womb, I sanctified you..." What is God saying here? God is simply telling Jeremiah that before he ever had life, he was elected and called for a specific assignment.

63

God calls you, just like Jeremiah, to seasons, hours and times to fulfill His purpose in your life, to get you to His destiny. But you will never get to the destiny of your life until you fulfill your purpose of the hour and of the season.

> **Before I formed thee in the belly I knew thee; and before thou camest forth out of the womb I sanctified thee, and I ordained thee a prophet unto the nations.**
>
> **Then said I, Ah, Lord GOD! behold, I cannot speak: for I am a child.**
>
> **But the LORD said unto me, Say not, I am a child: for thou shalt go to all that I shall send thee, and whatsoever I command thee thou shalt speak.**
>
> **Be not afraid of their faces: for I am with thee to deliver thee, saith the LORD.**
>
> **Then the LORD put forth his hand, and touched my mouth. And the LORD said unto me, Behold, I have put my words in thy mouth.**
>
> **See, I have this day set thee over the nations and over the kingdoms, to root out, and to pull down, and to destroy, and to throw down, to build, and to plant.**
> **Jeremiah 1:5-10**

Here, God went further to say, "I ordained you as a prophet to the nations even before you were born." In other words, God spoke Jeremiah's election into existence, formed it in His mind and when He communicated it to Jeremiah, He set him in order and got him started on his journey.

64

That is exactly what happens to every one of us. God spoke our election into existence even before we were born. Then He forms that election in His mind, and when He communicates it to us, He sets us in order and starts us on our journey. Election will always reveal your destiny.

Chapter Six

HOW TO ENTER INTO THE PURPOSE OF THE MANDATE

When God gives you a mandate or a promise in the form of a call or an election, that word will go through a progressive stage of metamorphosis. That word of promise goes from an imprint...to a representation...to a manifestation.

An imprint results when a mark or a figure is produced by pressure. It is an impression or picture of the original product. It is the negative of the original picture. The word of the Lord, when spoken over our life, is a seed. But that seed is just an imprint. It is not yet a representation of the tree or fruit of the tree. It is still at the messy stage. It needs to be properly sorted out, cleaned, observed and watered continually.

That is exactly what happens to the word of election that is spoken over our lives before the foundation of the earth. When God releases the word of promise to us, it immediately produces a mark. A mark which shows that we bear the promise. But the promise is still at the messy stage. It still needs to be sorted out properly and observed. This is the stage where a great deal of responsibility is required of us. You play a great role in the growth, development and maturity of the word of the Lord as it moves to the next level. This is the most delicate stage.

The second progressive stage is representation. After the word is imprinted, the imprinted word in us begins to grow and develop into a representation of what God has promised. A representation is the likeness or the model of that promise.

Finally, the mandate or promise becomes a manifestation of the promise or the word of the Lord. This is the stage when the word fully comes to pass in our lives.

JONAH'S EXPERIENCE

Now the word of the LORD came unto Jonah the son of Amittai, saying,

Arise, go to Nineveh, that great city, and cry against it; for their wickedness is come up before me.

But Jonah rose up to flee unto Tarshish from the presence of the LORD, and went down to Joppa; and he found a ship going to Tarshish: so he paid the fare thereof, and went down into it, to go with them unto Tarshish from the presence of the LORD.

But the LORD sent out a great wind into the sea, and there was a mighty tempest in the sea, so that the ship was like to be broken.

Then the mariners were afraid, and cried every man unto his god, and cast forth the wares that were in the ship into the sea, to lighten it of them. But Jonah was gone down into the sides of the ship; and he lay, and was fast asleep.

So the shipmaster came to him, and said unto him, What meanest thou, O sleeper? arise, call upon thy God, if so be that God will think upon us, that we perish not.

And they said every one to his fellow, Come, and let us cast lots, that we may know for whose cause this evil is upon us. So they cast lots, and the lot fell upon Jonah.

Then said they unto him, Tell us, we pray thee, for whose cause this evil is upon us; What is thine occupation? and whence comest thou? what is thy country? and of what people art thou?

Jonah 1:1-8

When God spoke to Jonah and told him "I want you to go to Nineveh," Jonah turned around and decided to go the other way. Why? Because he was afraid he would not to be able to accomplish the mandate of God upon his life. He decided to run away from God's mandate.

As he ran away, catastrophic events began to take place and these events began to affect innocent people around him because he was out of the will of God. That is exactly what happens to us and our environment when we are out of the

69

will of God, doing our own thing. The ship that carried Jonah was in chaos and disarray. The people were afraid. Their lives were in danger because of a rebellious, selfish individual who refused to fulfill the mandate of God upon his life. Somebody on the ship was out of the will of God. Somebody on the ship must be carrying a curse.

This is a powerful warning. The mandate of God is so important that when we are out of that mandate, we are exposed to the mandate of the enemy.

Jonah knew he had a call upon his life. He knew about it right from the beginning, but he blatantly refused it. He knew the reason things were not going well with the ship and with him was not because he was not praying, fasting or studying the word of God. He knew it was simply because he was out of the will of God.

God could have decided to take that word of promise from Jonah and give it to somebody else. But He did not. He could have found someone else that was a little more articulate, a little more willing or a little more talented to give it to. Why didn't He? Because it is not the soil that God keeps His eyes on. *He keeps His eyes on the seed.*

He does not look at your outer man. He does not look at your ability. He knows that once the seed is released, the corresponding ability to execute it will accompany it. But when He looks at you, He looks at the heart condition and says there is something inside of this person's make up, there is something inside of this person's character that I am

70

going to take and use. And it is this specific make up or character, not the anointing, that He is going to use to speak to the people of your generation.

That is why you must never desire to be like somebody else. God has fashioned your character and ordained it to accomplish His calling and mandate upon your life.

When God calls you, it is not by mistake. It is not something He pulls from someone else, but something that He gives to you specifically. He will chase after you. He will do everything He can to bring you to the place of the call. If you don't respond, the devil will eventually take you out. And only then is it given to someone else.

GOD SPEAKS ABOUT TOMORROW

For we have not followed cunningly devised fables, when we made known unto you the power and coming of our Lord Jesus Christ, but were eyewitnesses of his majesty.

For he received from God the Father honour and glory, when there came such a voice to him from the excellent glory, This is my beloved Son, in whom I am well pleased.
II Peter 1:16-17

When God speaks to you, He always speaks to you about the events that will take place in your life tomorrow. Why? So He can take you out of today and take you into tomorrow.

You receive honor and glory when God speaks to you. You can never get out of today unless you allow Him to reveal the glory of tomorrow. When Jesus Christ was on earth, God dealt with Him on receiving the glory of tomorrow. Twice, God spoke to Him and confirmed His glory. He said, "This is my beloved Son in whom I am well pleased." And immediately Jesus Christ began to see the glory of the resurrection.

We have a privilege that no other generation has, and that is we can have a divine revelation of that which lies beyond the veil of tomorrow. A prophetic generation knows what tomorrow holds. And the good news is that tomorrow does not hold defeat for the body of Christ. Tomorrow does not hold any failure for the body of Christ. When God gives you a glimpse into tomorrow, it is so He can take you out of today into tomorrow.

THE ROADBLOCK TO PURPOSE

Now is my soul troubled; and what shall I say? Father, save me from this hour: but for this cause came I unto this hour.

Father, glorify thy name. Then came there a voice from heaven, saying, I have both glorified it, and will glorify it again.

The people therefore, that stood by, and heard it, said that it thundered: others said, An angel spake to him.

Jesus answered and said, This voice came not because of me, but for your sakes.

72

Now is the judgment of this world: now shall the prince of this world be cast out.

John 12:27-31

Jesus Christ was doing fine with what the Father had assigned to Him until this point. In verse 27 of the above Scripture, Jesus Christ says that my soul is TROUBLED. The word "troubled" means "to be vexed." The word "vexed," on the other hand, means "to perplex the mind by suggesting doubt." Did Jesus doubt what His Father called Him to do? No, but there was a suggestion of doubt.

It was the same devil that, on a daily basis, comes against you, against your mandate. The word "vexed" also means "to suffer hurt, to be sad." It means "injury" and "to break." Satan was trying to get Christ into the place of perplexing the mind by suggesting doubt which would eventually cause Him to be sad, to break His focus, to suffer emotional hurt and injury.

Look at verse 27b. Jesus, as a result of His soul being troubled, said "what shall I say?" This is what has happened with the generation that has gone before us, and even some believers today. When their soul is troubled over what God has called them to do, the first thing they cry out or say is "I'm getting out of here." We want to escape that discomfort. We cry, "oh I want to go home." We get passive, lethargic and lazy.

But look at what Jesus said. He said "what shall I say about the perplexing of my soul." Look at His answer.

73

"Shall I say Father save me from this hour?" In other words, get me out of this call, this mandate, this thing that you have called me to do. Jesus did not say, "Father, get me out of here." Instead, He said "for this purpose I came." What purpose?

> **Father, glorify thy name. Then came there a voice from heaven, saying, I have both glorified it, and will glorify it again.**
>
> **John 12:28**

Jesus said, "Father, glorify your name." Then the purpose of Christ was revealed. This is one of the purposes of Christ: to release the voice of God from the heavens to the earth. When you make up your mind to fulfill the mandate of God upon your life and as you begin to fulfill it, you are releasing the voice of God from the heavenlies. God wants to be released in and through us.

RELEASING THE VOICE OF GOD

Why the need for the voice of God? The voice of God must be heard by a generation. If the voice of God does not come from heaven, there will be no shaking in the heavens and on earth. The Church needs to be shaken again. In the same verse 28, the Scripture says "then a voice came from heaven and God said I have glorified it and I will glorify it again." Listen to this. God says, I once glorified it in the past and I will glorify it again— tomorrow and in the future. The word "glory" means "to shine." God says once upon a time, in the past, I made you shine and now I am going to make you shine again.

Note the reaction of the people who were around Jesus. They were astonished, and some thought it was an angel. Jesus responded by telling the people that this voice did not come for Him but for them. He said, I heard it first at the baptism (the day of your calling is the day of your baptism). And I heard it again at the Mount of Transfiguration. This is a stage when you are serving your mandate with knowledge, understanding and vigor.

The second voice of God upon your life is for confirmation and usually to strengthen you in what He has spoken to you the first time.

TWO RESULTS OF THE VOICE OF GOD TO A PEOPLE

Now is the judgment of this world: now shall the prince of this world be cast out.
John 12:31

There are two things Christ said as a result of a voice coming to a generation or an individual who is serving the mandate of God. Verse 31 started by using the word "now." This word means "from this minute forth." From the very moment that the voice of God is released and heard, two things begin to take place.

First, the judgment of the world has begun. That is, God is demanding accountability and responsibility for what you are now aware that He has given you, or that He is doing. God says I will now hold you responsible and will judge you not as one in ignorance, but as one who knows what is expected of him.

The second result of the voice of God upon your life is that "now," from this minute forth, the rulers of this world will be cast out. The strongholds, the barriers and all of the impediments that the enemy has placed on your way to hinder you from entering the purpose of the mandate for your life are taken out. They are moved away.

There is something interesting about verse 31. It says "now the ruler of this world shall be cast out." The words "cast out" come from a Greek word which means "rapidly taunt and thump with repeated blows." In other words, rapidly beaten up with repeated blows. What this means is that when you receive the mandate of God upon your life and your soul gets vexed, you don't give up. Instead, you press in with the mandate, without crying "Lord get me out of here." The result: the mandate upon your life becomes activated and strengthened because of the voice of God that is released from the heavenlies.

From that moment forth, two things happen. First, judgment is released on earth against anything that would stand in the way of the mandate. Second, the ruler of this world (Satan and his cohorts) is rapidly taunted and thumped with repeated blows in every area of the mandate and your life where he decides to show up.

Chapter Seven

STAYING ON COURSE TO FULFILL THE MANDATE OF GOD

Once you successfully find the will of God, the mandate of God for your life, and you determine to serve that mandate with strength, a strong sense of destiny will be released in you. Along with the sense of destiny, five strong things will also begin to flow out of your life.

> **Do you not know that in a race all the runners compete, but [only] one receives the prize? So run [your race] that you may lay hold [of the prize] and make it yours.**
> **I Corinthians 9:24-27 (AMP)**

The first thing that flows out of a strong destiny is DISCIPLINE. A God-given vision produces discipline. When you know where God wants you to go, then you don't want to do anything that would get you off course. It produces not legalism or bondage, but a Godly discipline.

> **Where there is no vision [no redemptive revelation of God], the people perish; but he who keeps the law [of God, which**

includes that of man]— blessed (happy, fortunate, and enviable) is he.

Proverbs 29:18 (AMP)

For where your treasure is, there will your heart be also.
Matthew 6:21

The second thing a successful mandate will produce is VISION. Vision or direction comes out of a strong mandate. The Spirit of God will begin to produce a clear cut vision and strong direction in the execution of the mandate. The word "vision" originates from the word "optazion." It means "coming into view." According to the right timing, God begins to bring into view the appropriate elements of the mandate that area needed. As we walk strong into the mandate, the clearer the vision or direction is for our life.

THE PROVISION

Then said I unto them, Ye see the distress that we [are] in, how Jerusalem [lieth] waste, and the gates thereof are burned with fire: come, and let us build up the wall of Jerusalem, that we be no more a reproach.

Then I told them of the hand of my God which was good upon me; as also the king's words that he had spoken unto me. And they said, Let us rise up and build. So they strengthened their hands for [this] good [work].
Nehemiah 2:17-18

But my God shall supply all your need according to his riches in glory by Christ Jesus.
Philippians 4:19

80

The next thing that comes out of the mandate when you find it and follow it are FINANCES, resources and people. Money or resources follow vision. If you are having a money problem, it is because you are having a vision problem. Resources follow the vision, if God gave it. God only pays for what God orders.

This does not apply to church vision alone. It also applies to our daily desires in purchasing a home, a car or relocating when God did not tell you to. Ministries and individuals are suffering today because they ordered a vision and they are putting pressure on God to pay for it. God will not budge.

THE ENERGY AND DRIVE

Jesus saith unto them, My meat is to do the will of him that sent me, and to finish his work.
John 4:34

Look down from heaven, and behold from the habitation of thy holiness and of thy glory: where [is] thy zeal and thy strength, the sounding of thy bowels and of thy mercies toward me? are they restrained?
Isaiah 63:15

The fourth thing that will come when you begin to follow the mandate is ENERGY and DRIVE. What is energy? Energy is the inherent power. It is the power that helps you to operate. It is the strength of your expression and the potential ability to do work. The drive is simply the motivating urge that stimulates the response. It is the

81

propelling and forcible stroke that comes out of the urge. And every one of us needs the energy and drive to effectively finish the mandate of God.

Psalm 69:9 says that "the zeal of the Lord has eaten me up." In Isaiah 9:7, it says "the zeal of the Lord will perform this" and in II Corinthians 9:2, "your zeal provoked many." Throughout the scriptures you will find the key word "zeal." This zeal is the energy and drive that enables you to fulfill what God has ordained for you.

Finally, when you find out your mandate and begin to follow it, it will affect your self-esteem and self-worth. CONFIDENCE is built in you. You feel good about yourself. You feel good about what you believe in and what you are doing because you are doing what God made you to do and are being faithful in it. Discouragement hinders you when you don't know why you are here. I don't mind getting knocked down in a fight and getting back in the fight as long as I know that I am in the right fight. But I sure hate to know that I am in the wrong ring.

As a strong sense of destiny flows out of your life, it is very important to know how to stay on course concerning the mandate upon your life. Often people start the mandate, but lose the strength and the intensity of it because they do not know how to stay on course with what God has given them. The enemy will do everything possible to get you off course in the mandate, if for just a few minutes, to make you ineffective. So if you are going to stay on course with the calling of God upon your life, you must be willing to do some things.

STAYING FOCUSED

Brethren, I count not myself to have apprehended: but [this] one thing [I do], forgetting those things which are behind, and reaching forth unto those things which are before,

I press toward the mark for the prize of the high calling of God in Christ Jesus. Let us therefore, as many as be perfect, be thus minded: and if in any thing ye be otherwise minded, God shall reveal even this unto you.
Philippians 3:13-14

If any of you lack wisdom, let him ask of God, that giveth to all [men] liberally, and upbraideth not; and it shall be given him.

But let him ask in faith, nothing wavering. For he that wavereth is like a wave of the sea driven with the wind and tossed. For let not that man think that he shall receive any thing of the Lord. A double minded man [is] unstable in all his ways.
James 1:5-8

The first important way to stay on course is to stay focused. Have you ever seen a professional photographer? He is constantly adjusting the lens of his camera after every shot. Staying focused is single-mindedness. The word "focus" means "to concentrate." It means to be adjusted to a clear image. You cannot allow your mind or your will to be divided by more than one thing. A house divided against itself cannot stand. Don't waste your time on what does not apply to you.

I don't read books on fiction, not because they would not be entertaining, but I only have so much time and reading that material would not make the best use of it. There are things that I cannot do, not that they are wrong, but because I only have so much time. You need to invest in things that will help you. You cannot waste your time and money on activities and possessions that have no application to the direction of your life. You generally can look at the accumulations of a person and tell the direction of his life.

What do you waste your time on? Bonny Blair, the great Olympic skater, said that all her life, all she wanted to do was to skate. She concentrated and remained focused on it. She never turned right or left, and because of this she was able to accomplish her goal in life. What is it that you are good at which burns in your heart, that you have always wanted to do? You must be single-minded.

I have known people who have changed jobs several times. There is nothing wrong with changing jobs, but sooner or later you ought to find out what it is God wants you to do, buckle down and stay with it. Stay focused. People who lose it, always lose it in areas that are not their strength. Don't invest in areas that are not your strength. Always invest in areas of your strength. Don't ever get involved in something that is outside your strength, outside your expertise and outside your vision. It is a waste of precious time that you really don't have. Do one thing well, not a lot of things haphazardly.

THE ENEMY OF FOCUS

Wherefore seeing we also are compassed about with so great a cloud of witnesses, let us lay aside every weight, and the sin which doth so easily beset us, and let us run with patience the race that is set before us,

Looking unto Jesus the author and finisher of our faith; who for the joy that was set before him endured the cross, despising the shame, and is set down at the right hand of the throne of God.

For consider him that endured such contradiction of sinners against himself, lest ye be wearied and faint in your minds.

Hebrews 12:1-3

Focus has its enemies. These enemies are what the devil uses to throw you off focus. Your focus has a direct link with your energy or zeal. When a man loses his focus, he also loses his zeal, interest or energy for that thing. Often when Christians experience this, they make excuses why they are not doing what they are supposed to do. But the mature believer, or what I call the lover of God, realizes the cause and runs to God in prayer and fasting to adjust his vision lenses.

If you are going to stay focused, you must be willing to identify the enemies of your focus. You must be willing to sit down and write out those enemies that continually break your ministry focus, your financial focus, your marriage focus, your prayer focus. Why do you need to know your enemy? Because when you expose a liar, he can no longer lie to you.

WEIGHTS

Wherefore seeing we also are compassed about with so great a cloud of witnesses, let us lay aside every weight, and the sin which doth so easily beset us, and let us run with patience the race that is set before us
Hebrews 12:1

The first enemy of your focus is the enemy of weights. A weight is an amount of heaviness that produces pressure and burden. Many people are under the weights of finances. The reason the enemy puts weights on us is simply to take us off course. If he can disfocus you, he has successfully taken you off course.

There are different things in our lives that the enemy uses to exact these weights. The number one way is the weights that are produced through financial problems. Many times, when we are unable to pay our bills and meet our financial needs, it bothers us. We get discouraged and then concentrate on the problem, thereby taking our attention from the main agenda to which God has called us.

Second, weights are produced by sicknesses: sicknesses in our bodies and in the bodies of our loved ones. If a doctor tells you that you have a terminal disease, the enemy tends to take advantage of it to produce fear and doubt. These fears and doubts put a weight on you that would break your focus of what God has called you to do. The enemy's desire is for you to totally focus on what the doctor has told you.

Third, weights are produced through family problems, a loved one losing his job or the sudden death of a loved one. It might even be fighting among family members.

Finally, weights can be produced through ministry pressures. As a pastor of a growing church, I can understand this and relate to it. Weights are exacted when the finances are not coming in, when there is confusion and fighting among members or even leaders in the church.

EASILY BESETTING SINS

Wherefore seeing we also are compassed about with so great a cloud of witnesses, let us lay aside every weight, and the sin which doth so easily beset us, and let us run with patience the race that is set before us
Hebrews 12:1

The second enemy to our focus is the easily besetting sins. The word "beset" simply means "to take a step backward." The easily besetting sins are those things that the enemy succeeded in using against you the last time. These are sins that we are already familiar with...sins that we were once delivered from. These are sins that we have less resistance to. The enemy's target of attack in your life is always the place where he succeeded against you the last time. The distractions he used against you before are the ones that he keeps using.

The door which you left unlocked, that he can walk in and out of, is always the first place the enemy hits. It is not until you are able to identify where the leak is, that you can raise up a standard against the flood. If you cannot see the leak, you will never see the flood. Many of us have easily besetting sins— lies, lust, fornication, to name a few.

THE SPIRIT OF SHAME

The third enemy is the spirit of shame, the painful feeling that is caused by a sense of guilt or unworthiness. It is the disgrace, the humiliation, the misfortune and the outrage that is suffered by an individual. Shame is a paralyzing weapon that the enemy uses to destroy your emotions. It is this pain that knocks us off focus and prevents us from moving on with what God has ordained for our life.

THE FAINTING SPELL OF OUR MINDS

And let us not be weary in well doing: for in due season we shall reap, if we faint not.

Galatians 6:9

Have you not known? Have you not heard? The everlasting God, the Lord, the Creator of the ends of the earth, does not faint or grow weary: there is no searching of his understanding.

He gives power to the faint and weary, and to him who has no might he increaseth strength [causing it to multiply and making it to abound].

Even youths shall faint and be weary, and [selected] young men shall feebly stumble and fall exhausted:

But those who wait for the Lord [who expect, look for, and hope in him] shall change and renew their strength and power: they shall lift their wings and mount up [close to God] as eagles [mount up to the sun]: they shall run and not be weary, they shall walk and not faint or become tired.

                                    Isaiah 40:28-31 (AMP)

[The Servant of God says] the Lord God has given Me the tongue of a disciple and of one who is taught, that I should know how to speak a word in season to him who is weary. He wakens Me morning by morning, He wakens My ear to hear as a disciple [as one who is taught].

The Lord God has opened My ear and I have not been rebellious or turned backward.

                                    Isaiah 50:4-5 (AMP)

The final enemy to your focus is weariness and the fainting of our minds. One of the most frustrating things is to see what God promised you or spoke to you not coming to pass like we expect it to, and on time like we expect it. Often this makes us weary in believing if God will ever do it or even do those other things that He promised.

89

THE FORCE OF SUBMISSION

The second strategy to stay on course is to stay submitted to people that God places around you. Submission is simply an agreement to abide by the decision of an authority. The key word here is the word *agreement*. When we got born again, we went into an agreement called covenant and one of the terms of the agreement, of the contract, is to stay submissive to all authority, whether good or bad authorities. God has put life sources in our life not to hurt us, but to help us; to be checks and balances that will keep us from going beyond the borders He, God, set for our lives.

I hear so much today that submission is bondage or control. That is not true. Submission is actually liberty. It is an agreement to abide by the decision of an authority. Some people don't have a submissive spirit. They have an insubordinate spirit. A man who is submissive to a leader is a Christ-free man. But a man who rebels is a man who is Satan's servant.

[You who are] household servants, be submissive to your masters with all [proper] respect, not only to those who are kind and considerate and reasonable, but also to those who are surly (overbearing, unjust, and crooked).

For one is regarded favorably (is approved, acceptable, and thankworthy) if, as in the sight of God, he endures the pain of unjust suffering.

90

> [After all] what kind of glory [is there in it] if, when you
> do wrong and are punished for it, you take it patiently?
> But if you bear patiently with suffering [which results]
> when you do right and that is undeserved, it is acceptable
> and pleasing to God.
>
> For even to this were you called [it is inseparable from
> your vocation]. For Christ also suffered for you, leaving
> you [His personal] example, so that you should follow in
> His footsteps.
>
> **I Peter 2:18-21 (AMP)**

God did not tell us to just submit to nice leaders, to
calm leaders or to friendly leaders. He wants us to submit
to whatever leader is placed over us. A person who is
submissive is obedient. He finds it easy to obey. But a
person who is obedient is not necessarily submissive. He
may merely act submissive because of what he is getting—
money, food or even gifts.

> If the temper of the ruler rises up against you, do not leave
> your place [or show a resisting spirit]: for gentleness and
> calmness prevent or put a stop to great offenses.
>
> **Ecclesiastes 10:4 (AMP)**

God does not promote insubordination. This is an area
in which we have made major mistakes. Rather than doing
what the above Scripture says, we rise up against the leader
or the ruler, get upset with them and walk out saying, "well
I did not do anything to deserve that." Many Christians,
because of their stubbornness and rebelliousness, leave their
post before their harvest comes. It is very important that

91

God works in you a submissive spirit before you are placed in a leadership position.

STAY ON YOUR POST

And the Philistines gathered themselves together to fight with Israel, thirty thousand chariots, and six thousand horsemen, and people as the sand which [is] on the sea shore in multitude: and they came up, and pitched in Michmash, eastward from Bethaven.

When the men of Israel saw that they were in a strait, (for the people were distressed,) then the people did hide themselves in caves, and in thickets, and in rocks, and in high places, and in pits.
And [some of] the Hebrews went over Jordan to the land of Gad and Gilead. As for Saul, he [was] yet in Gilgal, and all the people followed him trembling.

And he tarried seven days, according to the set time that Samuel [had appointed]: but Samuel came not to Gilgal; and the people were scattered from him.

And Saul said, Bring hither a burnt offering to me, and peace offerings. And he offered the burnt offering.

And it came to pass, that as soon as he had made an end of offering the burnt offering, behold, Samuel came; and Saul went out to meet him, that he might salute him.

And Samuel said, What hast thou done? And Saul said, Because I saw that the people were scattered from me, and [that] thou camest not within the days appointed, and [that] the Philistines gathered themselves together at Michmash;

Therefore said I, The Philistines will come down now upon me to Gilgal, and I have not made supplication unto the LORD: I forced myself therefore, and offered a burnt offering.

And Samuel said to Saul, Thou hast done foolishly: thou hast not kept the commandment of the LORD thy God, which he commanded thee: for now would the LORD have established thy kingdom upon Israel for ever.

But now thy kingdom shall not continue: the LORD hath sought him a man after his own heart, and the LORD hath commanded him [to be] captain over his people, because thou hast not kept [that] which the LORD commanded thee.

I Samuel 13:5-14

In this Scripture, King Saul loses his kingdom because he stepped out of his authority and decided to walk as a priest. God said, "disqualified," and he lost the whole kingdom.

Learn to stay on your post or place of authority. God can only make you shine in your place of authority. That is always where your harvest resides. Stay submitted to the authority God puts in your life, whether natural authority or spiritual authority. If all of the God-given authority in your life is saying "no, no and no," don't do it. You'd better listen and obey to save your life. The authorities in your life are not placed there to hurt you, but to help you.

Many times we claim the devil attacked us after a life of disobedience. No, the devil did not attack you. Rebellion attacked you. The devil attacks good people. He does not attack rebels. Why? Because he doesn't need to. If you are rebellious, a nobody-tells-you-what-to-do kind of person, then no matter how great your destiny, you probably won't complete it because no one can talk to you.

YOUR SPHERE OF ANOINTING

Now after the death of Moses the servant of the LORD it came to pass, that the LORD spake unto Joshua the son of Nun, Moses' minister, saying,

Moses my servant is dead; now therefore arise, go over this Jordan, thou, and all this people, unto the land which I do give to them, even to the children of Israel.

Every place that the sole of your foot shall tread upon, that have I given unto you, as I said unto Moses.

From the wilderness and this Lebanon even unto the great river, the river Euphrates, all the land of the Hittites, and unto the great sea toward the going down of the sun, shall be your coast.

There shall not any man be able to stand before thee all the days of thy life: as I was with Moses, so I will be with thee: I will not fail thee, nor forsake thee.

Be strong and of a good courage: for unto this people shalt thou divide for an inheritance the land, which I sware unto their fathers to give them.

Only be thou strong and very courageous, that thou mayest observe to do according to all the law, which Moses my

servant commanded thee: turn not from it to the right hand or to the left, that thou mayest prosper whithersoever thou goest.

Joshua 1:1-7

The next way to stay on course with the mandate given to you is to stay within the boundaries of your call. A boundary is something that indicates limits. God has a limiting line of function for you and me.

Many Christians don't like to be limited. They want to be freelance Christians, allowed to do whatever they like to do. When you receive a calling, you must understand that God always gives a limiting line of function. After Joshua took over the reign and the leadership of Israel from his mentor Moses, God made absolutely clear the boundary of his function. God began by telling Joshua, "Every place that the sole of your foot shall tread upon, that have I given unto you."

That sounds like Joshua had a right to tread anywhere he willed. But that is not true. God went further to really clarify the prophetic word given to Joshua. He said it was only from "the wilderness and this Lebanon to the river Euphrates, including the land of the Hittites and to the great sea." God defined Joshua's boundaries. The anointing upon your life will function to its fullest capacity if you are operating within your allocated boundary.

There are some things in which you are not to be involved. Some of these things may be good, but they are not God things. I call them the forbidden fruit of your call. They become God things for you when they are included as part of your vision or mandate. If they are not, it is not a God thing for you. It might be for somebody, but not for you. You must not get involved in it. You must know your boundaries.

For example, you may be anointed to sing in your church's praise and worship team. The leader of that team may bring you up a couple times to sing and you may do an excellent job. But then all of a sudden you think your call is to have a national music ministry. What then happens is that you find yourself stepping out of your boundaries, and your finances, your marriage and other areas of your life begin to suffer because you just went beyond your boundaries. The people that God puts in your life as representatives to give balance, authority and direction may be saying "no" and you end up flat on your face.

Understand this: sometimes you can come under a corporate anointing of a vision and the Lord might allow your calling to shine because of the anointing that you are under. But because you do not understand the reason that your calling is shining, you think you can just go out and do it anywhere and expect the same result. God may not call you out to be a leader. He may call you to be part of a team--where you shine more as part of a team than just being on your own.

THE FORBIDDEN FRUIT OF YOUR BOUNDARY

He that diggeth a pit shall fall into it; and whoso breaketh an hedge, a serpent shall bite him.
Ecclesiastes 10:8

Within the boundary of your calling and mandate, God plants a forbidden tree that produces forbidden fruits. This tree and its fruit are always out of bounds. There is some forbidden fruit in our callings that we must not eat or tamper with. There are some things in our callings that we cannot touch. There are some places we cannot go. It is not legalism. It is because it is forbidden for my calling.

Your mandate is directly linked to your life. If it is forbidden for your call, it is also forbidden for your life. If you violate it, it can be detrimental to your life. The Bible in the above Scripture talks about the "hedge." A hedge is a fence that is built for protection against a loss. It is almost like a boundary that defines your space of protection. And when you break that boundary or hedge, the Bible says that a serpent shall bite you.

THE SECRET PLACE OF PROTECTION

He that dwelleth in the secret place of the most High shall abide under the shadow of the Almighty.

I will say of the LORD, [He is] my refuge and my fortress: my God; in him will I trust.

Surely he shall deliver thee from the snare of the fowler, [and] from the noisome pestilence.

97

He shall cover thee with his feathers, and under his wings shalt thou trust: his truth [shall be thy] shield and buckler.

Thou shalt not be afraid for the terror by night; [nor] for the arrow [that] flieth by day;

[Nor] for the pestilence [that] walketh in darkness; [nor] for the destruction [that] wasteth at noonday.
                              Psalm 91:1-6

The Scripture says "he that dwelleth in the secret place of the most high shall abide under the shadow of the Almighty." The secret place is the place of protection. It is the place of obedience in our lives to the will of God. As long as we are dwelling in there, we are safe and protected.

The mandate of God upon your life is your protection. When you are walking in the mandate of God for your life, there is a hedge or a fence of protection that is built around you. The place of obedience in your life becomes your secret place.

THE CONFIDENCE OF GOD

Now there was a day when the sons of God came to present themselves before the LORD, and Satan came also among them.

And the LORD said unto Satan, Whence comest thou? Then Satan answered the LORD, and said, From going to and fro in the earth, and from walking up and down in it.

And the LORD said unto Satan, Hast thou considered my servant Job, that there is none like him in the earth, a perfect and an upright man, one that feareth God, and escheweth evil?

Then Satan answered the LORD, and said, Doth Job fear God for nought?

Hast not thou made an hedge about him, and about his house, and about all that he hath on every side? thou hast blessed the work of his hands, and his substance is increased in the land.

But put forth thine hand now, and touch all that he hath, and he will curse thee to thy face.

And the LORD said unto Satan, Behold, all that he hath is in thy power; only upon himself put not forth thine hand. So Satan went forth from the presence of the LORD.

And said, Naked came I out of my mother's womb, and naked shall I return thither: the LORD gave, and the LORD hath taken away; blessed be the name of the LORD.

In all this Job sinned not, nor charged God foolishly.
                         Job 1:6-12,21-22

And the Lord turned the captivity of Job and restored his fortunes, when he prayed for his friends: also the Lord gave Job twice as much as he had before.

Then there came to him all his brothers and sisters and all who had known him before, and they ate bread with him in house; and they sympathized with him and comforted him over all the [distressing] calamities that the Lord had

brought upon him. Every man also gave him a piece of
money, and every man an earring of gold.

And the Lord blessed the latter days of Job more than his
beginning; for he had fourteen thousand sheep, six
thousand camels, one thousand yoke of oxen, and one
thousand female donkeys.

He had also seven sons and three daughters.

And he called the name of the first Jemimah and the name
of the second, Kezia, and the name of the third, Keren-
happuch.

And in all the land there were no women so fair as the
daughters of Job; and their father gave them inheritance
among their brothers.

After this Job lived one hundred forty years, and saw his
sons and his sons' sons, even four generations.

So Job died, an old man and full of days.
                                        Job 42:10-17(AMP)

The reason Job was protected was because he was in
the place where God wanted him, and he was willing to
stay there. God cannot force you into the mandate. You
must be willing to move into it and walk in it.

Job was willing to walk into the place of God--the
place of fulfillment, the place of the call--and the devil
could not touch him. Job's wife, children and friends were
not in the place of God and because of that, they did not
understand why Job needed to be faithful to God, in spite

of the attack of the enemy. The enemy can never be successful against us when we are operating in the boundary of our mandate. The only time he can touch us is when we are on his turf. As long as we are in the place of God--the mandate, the calling--we are in sync with life and are protected.

THE LURING TACTICS OF THE ENEMY

The devil knows this strategy. And because he knows it, he does everything possible to lure you out of that protective fence which is the will of God or the mandate of God for your life. He does it by trial, by frustration, by you giving up because you have not seen the promise of God yet come to pass. He lures you with an alternative, an Ishmael.

Now the serpent was more subtle than any beast of the field which the LORD God had made. And he said unto the woman, Yea, hath God said, Ye shall not eat of every tree of the garden?

And the woman said unto the serpent, We may eat of the fruit of the trees of the garden:

But of the fruit of the tree which is in the midst of the garden, God hath said, Ye shall not eat of it, neither shall ye touch it, lest ye die.

And the serpent said unto the woman, Ye shall not surely die:

For God doth know that in the day ye eat thereof, then your eyes shall be opened, and ye shall be as gods, knowing good and evil.

And when the woman saw that the tree was good for food, and that it was pleasant to the eyes, and a tree to be desired to make one wise, she took of the fruit thereof, and did eat, and gave also unto her husband with her; and he did eat.

And the eyes of them both were opened, and they knew that they were naked; and they sewed fig leaves together, and made themselves aprons.

Genesis 3:1-7

Look at the case of Adam and Eve, as long as they were in the garden following the instructions of God, the enemy would not have been able to deceive them. But when they entertained him, he was forced to be invited in.

Two powerful forces were used to lure them out of their place of protection: the first was *unbelief,* and the second, *lack of confidence in God.*

God [is] not a man, that he should lie; neither the son of man, that he should repent: hath he said, and shall he not do [it]? Or hath he spoken, and shall he not make it good?

Numbers 23:19

The devil was successful in getting Adam and Eve to disbelieve God. The enemy still uses this strategy today. If he can get us to disbelieve God, he can lure us out of our place of protection, out of the mandate of God for our lives.

The above Scripture declares the integrity of God, that He is not man and that He cannot lie. We must believe this. If He promises it, He will bring it to pass.

That is a comforting rock to rest upon. Man lies and cannot keep his promise. But God is not man, so He cannot lie.

Another force the enemy uses is the pressure to be like someone else. The enemy was able to lure Adam and Eve by developing within them an appetite to be like God. As long as they were satisfied in their place, they were secure and protected.

I believe this is a good lesson for us. We must be satisfied in our sphere of anointing because that is where our protection lies. Whenever we become dissatisfied, we begin feeling the pressure to be like someone else. Adam and Eve felt that pressure, and ended up being driven out of their Garden of Eden.

THE SAMSON DILEMMA

And there was a certain man of Zorah, of the family of the Danites, whose name was Manoah; and his wife was barren, and bare not.

And the angel of the LORD appeared unto the woman, and said unto her, Behold now, thou art barren, and bearest not: but thou shalt conceive, and bear a son.

Now therefore beware, I pray thee, and drink not wine nor strong drink, and eat not any unclean thing:

For, lo, thou shalt conceive, and bear a son; and no razor shall come on his head: for the child shall be a Nazarite unto God from the womb: and he shall begin to deliver Israel out of the hand of the Philistines.

Judges 13:2-5

The son Zorah's wife bore was Samson. Samson had a mandate upon his life, but he also had forbidden fruit attached to the call. There were things he would have to avoid if he was going to successfully serve the mandate of God.

Samson was called from the womb to be a Nazarite, a person set apart for God. He could not drink wine. He could not be associated with the dead and his hair could not be cut. As long as Samson did not eat of this forbidden fruit, the presence of God enabled him to execute the assignments of God. When Samson violated his mandate by allowing his hair to be cut off, he immediately lost the approval of God upon his life--and paid dearly for it.

And it came to pass afterward, that he loved a woman in the valley of Sorek, whose name was Delilah.

And the lords of the Philistines came up unto her, and said unto her, Entice him, and see wherein his great strength lieth, and by what means we may prevail against him, that we may bind him to afflict him: and we will give thee every one of us eleven hundred pieces of silver.

104

And Delilah said to Samson, Tell me, I pray thee, wherein thy great strength lieth, and wherewith thou mightest be bound to afflict thee.

And it came to pass, when she pressed him daily with her words, and urged him, so that his soul was vexed unto death;

That he told her all his heart, and said unto her, There hath not come a razor upon mine head; for I have been a Nazarite unto God from my mother's womb: if I be shaven, then my strength will go from me, and I shall become weak, and be like any other man.

And when Delilah saw that he had told her all his heart, she sent and called for the lords of the Philistines, saying, Come up this once, for he hath showed me all his heart. Then the lords of the Philistines came up unto her, and brought money in their hand.

And she made him sleep upon her knees; and she called for a man, and she caused him to shave off the seven locks of his head; and she began to afflict him, and his strength went from him.

Judges 16:4-6, 16-19

Samson allowed himself to be lured or enticed out of the favor of God. That is the enemy's strategy. He knows our weaknesses. He knows what captivates us. He uses that same weakness we've been aware of all our lives to lure us from the place of God--the place of the call, the election and your purpose.

Notice verse five,"...entice him and see in what his great strength lies and by what means we may overpower him, that we may bind him to subdue..." When the enemy entices us out of the mandate of God, he is able to find exactly where our strength lies. The enemy's plan, just as in Samson's life, is to lure us out of the will of God, to bind and subdue us with his spirit so we cannot return to the place of God's favor, thereby destroying the assignments of God upon our lives.

The enemy cannot destroy what God has entrusted into our hands if we are operating in the sphere of our anointing and refuse to eat the forbidden fruit of our tree. But bear in mind, as long as we are walking in the mandate of God, the enemy will persist. Verse 16 says, "she pressed him day after day." That is what the enemy does. He continually attempts to entice you out of the will of God.

So stand your ground. Know the good thing God has placed upon you. Refuse to bow to the pressure of enticement and God will honor you with a strong anointing.

You must fight to keep your calling pure. Otherwise, it will become polluted. You've got to be sold on what God told you to do. Be convinced every day that your call, your election and your purpose shall be established, that it will go into all the earth and it will survive. This is not pride. This is called *security*. When you become secure in your call, you will become sure in what God has told you to do. As you obey, doors of utterance will open to you and the anointing will increase.

ENDURANCE

Your next strategy to staying on course is patience, or endurance. This does not mean to sit idly by doing nothing. It means being steadfast, steady, consistent. Not giving up. Staying the course. You may have done everything right, but have not yet received the promise. So be patient and steadfast, doing it until you receive the reward. Wait. Don't give up. It will come.

Many people quit and get off course because they are not patient. They won't wait for the finished result after they have done the will of God. They are not healed yet. They have not received the financial breakthrough. The church has not grown yet. Stay with it until it happens.

Cast not away therefore your confidence, which hath great recompense of reward.

For ye have need of patience, that, after ye have done the will of God, ye might receive the promise.

For yet a little while, and he that shall come will come, and will not tarry.

Now the just shall live by faith: but if any man draw back, my soul shall have no pleasure in him.

But we are not of them who draw back unto perdition; but of them that believe to the saving of the soul.
Hebrews 10:35-39

Confidence is a force from God. Don't throw it away. Don't throw away your confidence that God is going to heal you. Don't throw away your confidence for that financial miracle.

The words "cast not away" come from a Greek word "*apoballo*," meaning "to throw away, to lose." In this Scripture, the reference is to "cowardly soldiers who throw away their weapons and flee from battle." Your confidence is a weapon given to you. It also is your shield. It has a protective function and, like soldiers, we must keep our weapon intact.

The word "confidence" is from the Greek word "*parrhesia,*" meaning "outspokenness." This word is translated as "boldness" in other scriptures. So this word confidence means "your boldness" or "your outspokenness in the full belief or trustworthiness of a person." Many Christians don't finish their mandate because they lack patience (endurance). They want everything now. God is doing something with every one of us while we wait on Him.

Often, we have the mentality, "Well, I have waited a week. I have fasted and prayed and confessed everything I know to confess, so where is it?" That is America. That is not Bible.

When a farmer plants a crop, he knows it is going to come up. He may not know exactly when, but he is confident the crop will appear in time. You have to know that God's promise of mandate is for eternity and life. When it is released or sown, it is going to come up.

TENACITY

The final strategy of staying on course with the calling, election and purpose of God is tenacity. Tenacity means "firmness in holding fast." It means keeping a firm hold, clinging or adhering persistently to something. It also means becoming adhesive to a thing...being "glued" to what you are called to.

> And he spake a parable unto them to this end, that men ought always to pray, and not to faint;
>
> Saying, There was in a city a judge, which feared not God, neither regarded man:
>
> And there was a widow in that city; and she came unto him, saying, Avenge me of mine adversary.
>
> And he would not for a while: but afterward he said within himself, Though I fear not God, nor regard man;
>
> Yet because this widow troubleth me, I will avenge her, lest by her continual coming she weary me.
>
> And the Lord said, Hear what the unjust judge saith.
>
> And shall not God avenge his own elect, which cry day and night unto him, though he bear long with them?

I tell you that he will avenge them speedily. Nevertheless when the Son of man cometh, shall he find faith on the earth?

Luke 18:1-8

I want you to see something in the Scripture above. The widow was a harmless Old Testament woman who had no authority, no clout, no way to intimidate. She wasn't married to anyone rich or famous. So she came to the big, bad judge and requested that he avenge her of her adversaries. At first, he refused. But afterward (days, months and years), he said to himself, "I am not afraid of God and I don't regard man. But this widow is driving me crazy. She is wearing on me."

Can you see the spirit of persistence here? And the Lord said in verse six, "Listen to what the unjust judge says." Now if Jesus tells us to listen, we'd better listen.

I tell you that he will avenge them speedily. Nevertheless when the Son of man cometh, shall he find faith on the earth?

Luke 18:8

Notice what the last part of the above verse says, "When the Son of Man cometh, will he find faith on the earth?" This Scripture has been misunderstood. In the Greek, it says simply, "when the Son of man cometh, will he find this kind of faith on the earth?" What kind of faith? *Tenacity.* Like a bull dog that won't let go. Faith that says, "I am going to hold you, Lord, to what You said. Not what I want. I won't let go. I won't back down. I won't give up."

110

The unjust judge avenged the widow woman because of her tenacity. True faith does not take *no* for an answer.

SPEAK TO YOUR MOUNTAIN

And Jesus answering saith unto them, Have faith in God.

For verily I say unto you, That whosoever shall say unto this mountain, Be thou removed, and be thou cast into the sea; and shall not doubt in his heart, but shall believe that those things which he saith shall come to pass; he shall have whatsoever he saith.

Therefore I say unto you, What things soever ye desire, when ye pray, believe that ye receive them, and ye shall have them.

Mark 11:22-24

We need to speak to our mountains. A lot of people talk about how big their mountains are, how much snow is on them, how slippery they are, how high they are and how nobody has ever climbed them. But God says don't talk about them. *Start speaking to them.* He said to rebuke them and command them to be cast away.

Don't tell people how big your mountain is. SPEAK the WORD OF GOD TO IT. What do you want it to do? A champion is a man who, when he stumbles, gets up and keeps getting up, no matter how often he stumbles.

Be tenacious with God. *And watch your mountain move!* Determine to STAY ON COURSE...be faithful in

111

your calling and purpose, and your God-given mandate will be fulfilled in your life.

MY PRAYER FOR YOU

Friend, I trust that, having read this book, you have a clearer understanding of God's divine destiny for your life. Now it's up to you to apply these principles and walk in your calling and purpose. If you want me to agree with you in faith that God will lead you from this point on, please pray along with me....

"Dear Heavenly Father, I thank You for the destiny You have placed upon my life. I thank You that I was called from birth to fulfill Your purpose and Your plan here on this earth. I know that I am "fearfully and wonderfully made," and am living in the right place at the right time.

Now in the Name of Jesus, I ask You to give me strength and determination to focus on my God-given mandate and stay on course to fulfill it. Fill me with Your grace and endurance, that I may be faithful in the small things. Help me to have a servant-attitude, so that YOU are the One who is glorified.

Father, help me to hear Your voice and obey Your instructions in every area of my life. Anoint me with Your Holy Spirit. Help me to be a blessing to all those around me, that they might see You.

In Jesus' Name, I come against the weights that would seek to sabotage the mandate on my life. I come against financial problems, sickness, weariness and those easily besetting sins that would distract me from realizing the fulness of Your glory. I ask You, Lord, to fill me with Your faith and favor.

113

Thank you for opening my eyes and my heart, Heavenly Father, to Your will in my life. Forgive me for those times I have strayed from the course or refused to follow Your call. I covenant with You now to listen and obey.

I love You, Father, and thank You for giving me a destiny, a purpose and a specific assignment for my life. In my own strength I am helpless, so I will depend upon You totally...to complete what You have begun in me. Use me for Your glory.

Thank you for hearing my prayer today. In Jesus' Name. Amen.

Now get happy and thank God for answering Your prayer. Praise and worship Him with all Your heart!

To request a complete catalog featuring books, video and audio tapes by Dr. John Tetsola, or to contact him for speaking engagements, please write, call or fax:

Ecclesia Word Ministries International
P.O. Box 743
Bronx, New York 10462

http://www.ecclesiaword.com

Phone (718) 904-8530
Fax (718) 904-8107